Cambridge Elements ≡

Elements in Public Policy
edited by
M. Ramesh
National University of Singapore (NUS)
Michael Howlett
Simon Fraser University, British Colombia
Xun WU
Hong Kong University of Science and Technology
Judith Clifton
University of Cantabria
Eduardo Araral
National University of Singapore (NUS)

ZOMBIE IDEAS

Why Failed Policy Ideas Persist

Brainard Guy Peters
University of Pittsburgh

Maximilian Lennart Nagel
Zeppelin University

T0287085

CAMBRIDGE
UNIVERSITY PRESS

CAMBRIDGE
UNIVERSITY PRESS

University Printing House, Cambridge CB2 8BS, United Kingdom

One Liberty Plaza, 20th Floor, New York, NY 10006, USA

477 Williamstown Road, Port Melbourne, VIC 3207, Australia

314–321, 3rd Floor, Plot 3, Splendor Forum, Jasola District Centre,
New Delhi – 110025, India

79 Anson Road, #06–04/06, Singapore 079906

Cambridge University Press is part of the University of Cambridge.

It furthers the University's mission by disseminating knowledge in the pursuit of
education, learning, and research at the highest international levels of excellence.

www.cambridge.org
Information on this title: www.cambridge.org/9781108926034
DOI: 10.1017/9781108921312

First published 2020

A catalogue record for this publication is available from the British Library.

ISBN 978-1-108-92603-4 Paperback
ISSN 2398-4058 (online)
ISSN 2514-3565 (print)

Zombie Ideas

Why Failed Policy Ideas Persist

Elements in Public Policy

DOI: 10.1017/9781108921312
First published online: November 2020

Brainard Guy Peters
University of Pittsburgh

Maximilian Lennart Nagel
Zeppelin University

Author for correspondence: B. Guy Peters, bgpeters@pitt.edu

Abstract: Ideas are important in shaping the policy choices of governments. But many ideas that have not been successful in the past continue to be used by policymakers, and some good ideas tend not to be adopted. This Element will focus on why governments make these poor policy choices. We will discuss a number of examples of "zombie ideas" that refuse to die, and then discuss the factors that are associated with their survival. Those factors occur at the elite, the organizational and the societal levels. We will also examine some "ghost" ideas that may well be successful but have a difficult time being adopted, and the factors that are associated with the exclusion of these ideas from the policy process.

Keywords: policy ideas, policymaking, path dependence, blame avoidance, elites

ISBNs: 9781108926034 (PB), 9781108921312 (OC)
ISSNs: 2398-4058 (online), 2514-3565 (print)

Contents

Practical men, who believe themselves to be quite exempt from any intellectual influences, are usually slaves of some defunct economist.

John Maynard Keynes, *The General Theory of Employment, Interest and Money* (1936)

A misconceived theory can kill.

Amartya Sen, *Beyond the Crisis: Development Strategies in Asia* (1999)

As a dog returns to its vomit so does the fool repeat his folly.

Proverbs 26:11

The adoption of public policies reflects a number of influences of the actors charged with making those difficult choices (see Peters, 2016, chapter 2). Policies often reflect the power of interests in the society, especially business. Policy choices are also influenced by the nature of the institutions within which they are made, and the interactions of those public sector institutions with other social and political institutions. Increasingly, policy choices are influenced by the international environment and the pressures of both global markets and global governance structures. And, at times, policy choices may be a matter of the individual preferences of actors within the process.

In this Element, however, we will focus on the role of ideas in shaping public policy choices. While the influence of ideas on actual policy choices may at times be difficult to track, no policy exists without ideas. There must be some underlying idea, first, that there is a policy problem (Rochefort and Cobb, 1994) that requires action, and, second, that there is a means of solving that problem. The process of policy formulation (Jordan and Turnpenny, 2015) or policy design (Peters, 2018) involves bringing ideas to bear on policy, first in the conceptualization of the problem and then in the conceptualization of the solution.

Indeed, most processes of policy formulation or policy design will involve several levels of ideas about solving the underlying problem. There must be some idea about a general approach to the problem – perhaps thinking in terms of Christopher Hood's (1984) familiar NATO categories. Then, a more refined and precise set of ideas will be required to address the problem. There may be some agreement that "Treasure" based instruments are appropriate for addressing a problem, but then a choice must be made among subsidies, tax-based instruments or grants. And then that choice must be refined even further. All of those instrument choices involve an idea of how the economy and society function, and how best to intervene.

Policy analysis also involves applying values to the outcomes of the policy process. Are those outcomes good or bad, acceptable or unacceptable, and on what basis are they to be evaluated? This type of normative analysis in public policy involves the use of ideas as a foundation of the analysis (see Campbell, 2002; 23–5). Sometimes those ideas are not very explicit, as in the utilitarian assumptions underlying cost–benefit analysis (McIntyre, 1992). But in formalized policy evaluation (Vedung, 2013) the ideas being used to assess policy are generally quite explicit – and need to be so, for a transparent analysis of policy. Policy analysis is, even with all the development of statistical and formal techniques, still a normative enterprise involving ideas and values.

This Element is not about how bad ideas about public policy are created in the first instance. There is already an extensive literature about the existence of bad ideas in a number of policy domains. The prevalence of faulty ideas has perhaps been clearest in foreign policy (see Walt, 2005), but there has been no shortage of poor ideas in domestic policy as well. The nature of those bad ideas has been examined in some detail (see Hogwood and Peters, 1985; Bovens and 't Hart, 1998; 2016; King and Crewe, 2013). Nor is this Element a condemnation of ideas that persist just because they persist. Some of those continuing political ideas are essential for governance, especially democratic governance (Lacorne, 2016), and can legitimate policymaking in the public sector. Additionally, some substantive policy ideas that have persisted for decades may remain valuable approaches to the policy problems in question. The pandemic of 2020 has illustrated that the old public health ideas of quarantine and contract tracing continue to have substantial validity.

In this Element we will not be dealing with the persistence of policy ideas for administrative reform within government, although much of the same logic is apparent when those ideas are presented and adopted. There are many "convenient" ideas for governments to use when they are faced with a governance problem. For example, decentralization has been a common response to governance problems in many countries, just as recentralization has been after decentralization fails to produce the desired outcomes. In this presentation, however, we will focus more on substantive policy areas rather than administrative reform.

Finally, we are not concerned with policy ideas that are adopted simply to respond to "policy traps." Political leaders may well know that the policies they advocate are likely to be ineffective (McConnell, 2019), but adopt them because they need to do *something* in the face of popular demands or a genuine crisis. We would only become interested in these policy traps if they are set and sprung repeatedly and produced the same results. In that case they would represent the persistence of ineffective ideas – or "zombie ideas," in our terms.

This Element will first discuss briefly the literature on policy ideas and their influence on public policy. We will then develop the concept of "zombie ideas" to describe policy ideas that, although largely unproven in practice, tend to survive and to be adopted again and again (see also Krugman, 2019; 2020). This discussion will also, to some extent, discuss the provenance of bad policy ideas more generally, although much of the literature on ideas and policy tends to be more positive (see Mehta, 2011). Finally, we will discuss the logic for the persistence of these zombie ideas, even in an era in which evidence-based policymaking is meant to be the norm in the public sector.

1 Policy Ideas and Public Policies

We do not have the space available here to rehearse the extensive literature on the role of ideas in public policy. As Lord Keynes argued some years ago, however, ideas do have an influence, and they may persist long after their utility has waned and the sources of the ideas have themselves become defunct. In this discussion of policy ideas, we will utilize Béland and Cox's (2011, 2; Béland, 2019) conception of ideas as "causal beliefs." This conception is especially useful in thinking about policy design because it points out that any policy design is making an assumption about causation, whether implicitly or explicitly (Peters, 2021). Further, an idea may not have a strong empirical foundation but can be a belief, a point to which we will return later.

Ideas come into play in policy analysis in a variety of ways. One of the more common of these is framing, in which an observed problem in the society is framed in a certain way in order to make it amenable to a given solution. Framing involves the use of ideas, or perhaps the creation of ideas, in order to shape the problem in a way that can be processed by the political system and processed in the ways desired by the framers. Problems do not really exist, in policymaking terms, until they have been framed, and the way in which they are framed will determine the type of solution which is likely to be applied to the problem (see Pierce et al., 2004).

Ideas about public policy may exist at a variety of levels. Some reflect the existence of large-scale ideologies, such as Marxism or neoliberalism, that are attempts to provide meaning for, and solutions to, almost the entire spectrum of political problems. Ideas may also exist at a meso level – for example, the difference between Keynesianism and monetarism as solutions for economic issues. And, finally, policy ideas may exist at a micro level. For example, individuals and organizations may have commitments to particular policy instruments as the best way to solve almost any policy problem (see Linder and Peters, 1989; 1992).

The ideas that affect policies have also been discussed in the literature as "policy paradigms" that guide action for a period of time (Hall, 1993). This concept is now widely used to describe the way in which ideas influence policy choices, although the exact mechanisms through which that influence is exerted may not be clear (Daigneault, 2014). But the use of the term "paradigm" indicates that these ideas are assumed to have a rather pervasive impact, to survive for some time and also to be largely unquestioned. These unquestioned assumptions are used by the policymakers who invoke them to guide their policy choices and to explain those choices to the public. As Frans Leeuw has written:

> A policy theory is a system of social and behavioral assumptions that underlie a public policy which have been formulated in the form of propositions. These propositions reflect beliefs of policy makers about the cognitions, attitudes and behaviors of the policy's target group: the people whom the policy is to affect. But they also refer to more structural factors on which policy makers have been making assumptions. (Leeuw, 1991: 74)

The notion of a policy paradigm, if we follow the conceptualization of paradigms by Thomas Kuhn (1962), implies a dominant approach to a domain of science for Kuhn, or to a policy domain in our analysis of public policy. In both instances the paradigm will dominate thinking and action, and actors committed to the paradigm will fight to maintain the paradigm in the face of criticism and negative evidence. Only when there is an alternative paradigm that can clearly do a better job than the existing paradigm is change likely to occur.

As we think about the role of ideas in policy analysis it is important to consider how they interact with other possible explanations of policy choices. For example, ideas may simply be a form of rationalization or justification of self-interest (Rodrik, 2014). Expressing blatant self-interest may be considered somewhat unseemly, so some justification must be developed to validate the pursuit of that self-interest. Policy ideas are the obvious source for those justifications. One cannot say that a tax cut will help me and my rich friends, but one can say that tax cuts will increase economic growth or increase economic freedom for all citizens.

In addition to the self-interest of the policymaker, policy ideas may reflect the preferences of interests within the society. Political leaders may be the repository of ideas and may also feed ideas from their political parties into the policy process. But unions, business groups, conservation groups and other social actors can introduce policy ideas into the process. And some of these ideas may be zombie ideas that have been proven politically, if not substantively, invalid. The ideas of previous Labour manifestoes, such as those from the campaigns of Michael Foot and Neil Kinnock, were brought into the campaign of Jeremy Corbyn by Momentum and other Left organizations and unions, to no good effect for the Party's electoral outcome in 2019.[1]

---

[1] In fairness, Corbyn would have advocated, and did advocate, very similar ideas all on his own, but the links with party history may have helped legitimate those ideas within the party (Riley, 2019).

Also, we must remember that ideas can be an impediment to effective policymaking, as well as a boon. This is especially true when there is a need to coordinate policies and those policies are based on different ideas (Schön and Rein, 1994; see also Bardach, 1997). When individuals have deeply held policy beliefs, they can find working with others who do not share those beliefs difficult, and especially so if the second party also has different beliefs. Thus, while ideas may give guidance for policy choices, they can also make bargaining and compromise – almost inevitable features of the policy process – more difficult.

Policy ideas or symbols can prevent action as well as lead to actions. Some strong policy ideas can place a mortmain on action and make it almost unthinkable for policymakers to act in certain ways. During the Cold War era, foreign policy ideas that denigrated any form of appeasement, and acceptance of the "domino theory" (see Section 2.8) prevented adopting more innovative approaches to foreign policy. Likewise, the specters of "communism" and "socialism" were used to slow down social policy reforms in some Western countries. In these cases, the presence of zombie ideas may have been associated with the creation of more "ghost ideas" – good ideas that were never adopted.

And, finally, some policy ideas can be too powerful, and produce overreactions from government (Maor, 2012). Even good policy ideas, meaning those that are capable of producing the desired outcomes from the policy process, may not be used proportionately, producing waste or perhaps even undermining the success of a program. Using a medical metaphor, Hogwood and Peters (1985) referred to this type of over-reaction as "choking."

Although ideas are inevitably involved in making policies, some ideas are more powerful and can produce better results than others. Some policy ideas may be discussed for years and never be adopted or implemented, while others are tried again and again. Some policy ideas, when adopted, fail to produce the results expected by their advocates – and may even fail to deliver any positive results at all. And some policy ideas may be successful, yet not persist and soon be forgotten. Table 1 presents a simple typology of policy ideas based on their success and their persistence.

The two cells in this typology labeled "winners" and "losers" are what one might expect to see when observing policymaking over time. Ideas that demonstrate that they are related to policy success continue to be adopted, while those that do not work are abandoned. The other two categories are more interesting. This Element will focus on those "zombie ideas": ideas that refuse to die even after they have been proven unlikely to produce successful interventions. We will later turn our attention briefly to "ghost ideas": those

Table 1 The Success of Policy Ideas and Their Survival

		Continued Use of Ideas	
		Yes	No
Success of Policies Based on Ideas	Yes	Winners	Ghost Ideas
	No	Zombie Ideas	Losers

that seem likely to produce success, but which are never, or rarely, adopted (see Section 3.2.12) [2]

Jeffrey Legro (2000) has addressed a relatively similar question concerning policy ideas, which he characterizes as "collective ideas." However, he looks only at policies that are adopted, regardless of their conformity to the prevailing collective ideas. He argues that when policies that are prescribed by the prevailing ideas fail, the ideas will be forced to change. This assumption that the feedback from failure will produce change in policies and policy ideas appears to be common within policy studies and political science.

We, however, argue that the assumption of learning and changes in policy ideas is questionable. Indeed, quite the opposite appears to occur in many cases, and we posit that policy ideas (collective ideas) may persist even when they are not successful. We will provide some examples of policies that have failed even though the ideas that provided their justification continue to be accepted among at least part of the political community. Our question, then, is how can these policy ideas survive when logically they should be discarded?

We have been using words like "bad" or "poor" synonymously to describe policy ideas, and will continue to do so. We do not mean that those ideas are evil or likely to produce harmful outcomes. We mean that they will produce no outcomes, or not nearly the level of benefit assumed by their proponents. And when we discuss "bad" ideas we are not interested in programs that fail because of poor implementation or because of inadequate investment of resources. Many good ideas – that is, those for which the causal belief may be fundamentally sound – may fail because of inadequate resources or limited implementation capacity,

In summary, ideas do matter for policy. Public policies may reflect the wishes of powerful social and economic interests, and they may reflect the political

---

[2] Thanks to Ben Cashore for the term "ghost ideas," and for his numerous helpful suggestions on the Element.

power of individual leaders, but they tend to be justified and explained through ideas. And ideas may be more persistent than individuals or even specific interests, and, once adopted as "ideas in good currency" (Schön, 2010), may continue to influence decision-makers for some time. Indeed, Schön argued that although the ideas that shape policies will change, they often lag behind changes in the policymaking environment, and hence the existence of zombie ideas may be endemic in policymaking. But then the question becomes why they persist? And are there differences in the learning capacities of governing systems that contribute to shorter or longer time lags (Peters, 2014)? First, we must clarify more fully exactly what we mean by zombie ideas.

2 What Do We Mean by Zombie Ideas?

As mentioned, by "zombie ideas," we mean ideas that will not die, no matter how often they are disproved.[3] That is a rather strong statement, given that it is difficult to say that any idea has failed, unequivocally, and indeed there are questions about what actually constitutes policy failure (McConnell, 2010). Also, we can only say that the policies have not been abandoned up to a certain point in time, but not that they will not be dismissed in the future. Yet it is also clear that some ideas continue to return to the active policy agenda with little evidence to support them, and at times even after very poor performance of policies designed around them.

We also recognize that some of the policy ideas we have labeled as zombie ideas may have had some positive effect at some points in time, and in some places. However, we argue that these ideas have become so ingrained in the policymaking systems that they may be adopted without adequate thought, even when they are not useful or may be counterproductive. Some zombie ideas are misguided from the time they are first adopted, but most have had some utility before becoming the policy choices of first resort, regardless of their utility at present.

It is also important to say what zombie ideas are not. Most importantly, we should emphasize that zombie ideas are not just bad ideas, even if those bad ideas are popular and widely diffused at one point in time. For example, the idea of prohibiting the sale and consumption of alcohol was very popular in the late nineteenth and early twentieth centuries (see Schrad, 2010), with a number of countries adopting prohibition. The policies based on that idea were not successful in eliminating the use of alcohol, and there were numerous negative externalities from the programs. This idea for regulating alcohol was relatively

---

[3] We acknowledge that several economists, notably Paul Krugman (2019) and John Quiggin (2013), used the term "zombie ideas" either before or at about the same time as we did. But their discussions have focused more on describing the phenomenon than attempting to explain it, and not on explaining it in political terms.

short-lived, however, and is now largely considered to have been a major policy mistake. That said, critics of the prohibition of "soft drugs" argue that this type of policy thinking persists, and we will discuss that example in Section 2.7.

Also, we are more concerned with the persistence of ideas that do not produce the desired changes in the economy and society than we are with policies that have numerous negative side effects or which may produce the desired effects only at great cost. For example, the Interstate Highway System in the United States did achieve its basic goal of making driving around the country easier, but it did so at great social and environmental cost. These highways made moving out of cities easier and fostered both the decline of inner cities and increased gasoline use in commuting. This may have been a bad policy, but it is not necessarily a zombie policy even if highways continue to be a common "solution" to transportation problems.

We will give several examples of zombie ideas in this section of the Element. These are drawn to great extent from the American and German experiences, but some have infected policymaking in other settings as well. Further, this sample of ideas is drawn largely from the political and ideological Right, but there are some from the Left that are mentioned as well. And, as we point out (see Section 3.1), while some of these ideas may be justifications for self-interest on the part of the individuals advocating them, they are still important given the extent to which they may influence policy choices. Justification through a zombie idea may enable a political interest to implement its program, even if it may in the end produce disappointing results.

2.1 Tax Cuts Produce Economic Growth

Perhaps the most enduring zombie idea in American politics is that tax cuts will easily produce economic growth (Jones and Williams, 2008). The usual way in which this idea has been expressed in practice has been a "trickle-down" approach in which tax cuts for the wealthy and for corporations will lead to their investing and spending more money, which in the long-run will produce economic growth that will help the less affluent in society. Even the Kennedy tax cuts of the 1960s were assumed to operate somewhat like this, even though the changes made in the tax system were more equitable than those of Reagan and Trump.

There are at least two codicils to this general idea of tax cuts being a sure instrument for achieving economic growth. The first, and more famous, is the Laffer Curve. Propounded by the economist Arthur Laffer[4] during the Reagan

---

[4] The story, perhaps apocryphal, is that the idea was first propounded on a napkin at lunch with some economic advisors to President Reagan.

presidency, the argument was that tax cuts will pay for themselves by creating enough economic growth that even lower tax rates will produce as much government revenue as before the cuts (see Peacock, 1989). This claim resurfaced in the discussions of the Trump tax cuts, although the soaring federal deficit during that administration (even before the coronavirus pandemic struck) appeared to be good evidence that the notion is as wrong now as it was for Ronald Reagan.

The second codicil to the general argument that tax cuts produce economic growth is the notion of supply-side economics – or, in George H. W. Bush's term, "voodoo economics."[5] While Keynesian economics largely depends upon manipulating demand, supply-side economics, as the name implies, depends on manipulating supply. That is, it depends on investment that results from tax cuts, and possibly other concessions to business, and which will in turn produce more jobs and higher income for workers As is true for this general line of argument, there are seemingly faulty behavioral assumptions on the supply side.[6] It appears, for example, that much of the Trump tax cut for the wealthy has gone to consumption by individuals and stock buy-backs by corporations (Coy, 2018) rather than to investment.[7]

In addition to the assumptions about the efficacy of tax cuts, for the United States the use of the tax code as a general policy tool to achieve the distribution of benefits as well as the collection of revenue can be seen as a zombie idea used by both the Left and the Right (see Irwin, 2020). For example, several of the more important provisions of the Affordable Care Act (Obamacare) were implemented through the tax system, rather than as direct health expenditures. While tax expenditures ("loopholes") may be less visible to voters than are direct expenditures, those political benefits are offset by the difficulty in targeting tax benefits as effectively as expenditures. But the practice persists, and continues to expand, in large part because it is now part of the accepted practice of governing and in part for political convenience.

2.2 Work Requirements on Social Programs Move People into More Productive Lives

Another neoliberal zombie idea has been "workfare" or, more politely, "welfare to work" programs (see Quaid, 2002). These programs have the requirement that individuals receiving social benefits engage in some form of productive activity, and preferably in paid employment. These programs have been

---

[5] It is the rare academic thesis that can include both zombies and voodoo.

[6] The supply-side version of economic policy has a long history, in the United States and elsewhere. See Campbell and Anderson (2001).

[7] For a general discussion, see Schmidt (2016).

implemented in a number of countries, including some that have been historical champions of the welfare state. They have also been evaluated extensively, with the general conclusion being that at best they have minimal effects, other than reducing the level of participation in the programs (Greenberg and Cebulla, 2008).

The German Hartz IV reform serves to illustrate this argument. Since it came into force in 2005, welfare benefits and unemployment insurance have been discussed extensively. This reform was introduced by a coalition government led by the Social Democratic Party (SPD) in 2003. When you lose your job, you are required to attend meetings with advisors, have to prove that you are looking for a new position, or have to enroll in training. If you refuse a job offer, your advisor can stop the support; if you miss a meeting, your benefits may be cut. The German welfare system now provides a sociocultural minimum payment for living. Hartz 4 is designed to nudge recipients of social welfare into employment, even if the job doesn't match a recipient's qualifications or is poorly paid. Since Hartz 4 entered into force, Germany's unemployment rate was low, and reached its lowest level since 1949 in 2016. But the reform has been criticized. Accordingly, "the coercive provisions of Hartz IV are seen as a way of humiliating the unemployed and squeezing the poor" (see Zimmermann, 2017). Ironically, a social-democratic and pro-labor party paved the way for one of the most controversial and neoliberal reforms of recent decades.

While "welfare to work" programs may have had some virtues as a means of gaining job experience, the extension of Medicaid under the Trump administration (Kaiser Health Network, 2019) represents a policy idea that has clearly lived too long.[8] The evidence concerning the population receiving Medicaid is that only a limited number of the individuals on Medicaid who are not working could work with any significant economic benefit. A large proportion of Medicaid participants are elderly or are children, and many of working age are disabled. Most of the remainder are already working, albeit for low wages and for employers who do not provide health insurance. Leaving aside the question of whether the program might actually motivate the few people who could work, the program is designed more to make a political and ideological point than to actually shape health policy.

A similar requirement for work in order to receive Supplemental Nutrition Assistance Program benefits (SNAP, or "Food Stamps") has been projected to actually cost the federal government money, rather than saving money

---

[8] Medicaid is medical insurance for the indigent. The income limits for eligibility are determined by the individual states, but most of the funding is federal.

(Linderman, 2019), through reducing the number of participants. A lack of adequate nutrition would impose costs in Medicaid programs and other social programs. These costs are in addition to the additional costs that would be imposed on state and local governments, and private charities, by work requirements to receive Food Stamps. And, in the short term, those costs may pale in comparison to the long-term social costs of poor nutrition for thousands of children during their formative years.

Workfare rules of social policy do help demonstrate one of the most important conceptual and methodological issues in zombie ideas. This problem is that many policies have more than one objective, and although a policy may fail in terms of one aim, it may still succeed on one or more other of its goals. For example, for work requirements being required for social policy benefits, the stated goal is to get people off benefits and back into gainful employment. The other goals are perhaps simpler, if unstated – simply removing people from the programs and saving government money. These programs are generally successful in terms of the second goal, yet rarely on the first, more visible goal. Are they failures?

2.3 Privatization of Public Services

The New Public Management reform movements in the global context were decisively influenced by the municipal budget crises of the 1980s and 1990s, which also led to demands for structural and control changes. In this context, the first Kohl government in 1982 in Germany also played an important role. The loss of the SPD's chancellorship meant a move away from social-liberal politics and toward more conservative-liberal policies (Wollmann, 2002). In the neo-liberal style of Thatcher and Reagan, in his first government declaration Kohl proclaimed a reorientation of the public sector and declared "[a] return the state to its original and real tasks, while at the same time ensuring that it can fulfil them reliably" (Jann and Wewer, 1998: 229). On the same token, financial consequences of the reunification have had a lasting influence on the budgets of West German municipalities because of the need to support East German municipalities.

Röber (2018) distinguishes six kinds of privatization. Only the material one is crucial for this Element. So-called material privatization occurs when state-owned enterprises are moved from the public to the private sector (i.e., the selling of state-owned properties to private interests). Private businesses carry out public goods and become important social actors. Popular examples can be found in the UK, USA, Germany and many other states. Among the best-known cases in the UK under Thatcher were the privatizations of Britoil, British-Gas and regional water authorities. The question became whether the service "has to be provided itself" or whether it can be carried out by a private actor.

Throughout the 1980s, 1990s and early 2000s, Germany faced privatizations at the national, federal and local levels. Shifting the perspective toward the local and municipal levels, various examples can be found. Local water authorities and electrical utilities, public transport and even public housing associations were sold out to the private sector. Such trends emphasize the idea that privatizations will increase both a government's efficiency and its quality, shrink the size of government and reduce taxes in general. Accordingly, citizens theoretically benefit from privatizations because of the profit-seeking behavior of private managers. Such behavior is supposed to increase customer satisfaction and decrease costs for customers.

Yet, after years of reform euphoria there is a certain disappointment over the possibilities of management-oriented reforms within the public sector. Rather, there is a trend toward a remunicipalization of privatized tasks. Berlin, for instance, followed a popular vote and bought back its electrical utilities and power generation. Accordingly, private managers were not acting in the public's interest, prices were rising, and customer satisfaction was low. Many more examples can be found in Germany, highlighting that privatization is not panacea. Privatization incorporates various problematic aspects that need to be taken into consideration. And even though we have learned that the hard way, the panacea named privatization is still extolled and demanded by practitioners and scholars.

2.4 Industrial Policy and Innovation

The mirror image of the idea of privatization assumes that the public sector can make more effective decisions about innovation in the economy than can the market itself. This has been the foundation of industrial policy in a number of settings, and continues to be a part of the standard economic policy for many political parties of the Left. The assumption is that market actors have too-limited a conception of what a good investment may be and fail to take into account social benefits that may accrue along with strictly economic benefits. In addition, governments may want to consider the geography of investments more than would actors in the private sector, attempting to improve conditions in economically deprived parts of the country.

The well-established literature on Varieties of Capitalism (Hall and Soskice, 2001) differentiates between coordinated and liberal market economies. Soskice (1999) argues that liberal market economies are better in coping with radical innovations (Schröder, 2014). While incremental innovations are easy for the coordinated market economies to adopt, flexible, risky innovations are not. The involvement of state interests, and the political interests that are behind them, slows innovation processes.

The problem has been that industrial policies tend not to work as effectively as their advocates would like to think (but see Peneder, 2017). First, there is a political tendency to use industrial policies to maintain existing "sunset" industries rather than to invest in "sunrise" industries. The established industries have workers (and voters) that government does not want to offend. Likewise, governments may be more risk averse than are some entrepreneurs, and perhaps rightly so. Government industrial policies are using money from the taxpayers, who may not like that money to be used in a risky manner.

That having been said, there may be instances in which industrial policies may have some virtues, but they have been largely terminated by changes in policy ideas. It can be argued that industrial policies can be very useful devices for developing countries that need to use the power of the state to mobilize capital and to protect new industries from international competition (Altenburg and Lütkenhorst, 2015). And industrial policies were certainly effective in the development of the "Little Tigers" in Asia, although these countries have now largely moved away from that strategy as its effectiveness has declined (Stubbs, 2009). Thus, as argued earlier, some zombie ideas may have been effective when first implemented. As their utility diminishes, they may continue to be implemented without much conscious thought because the idea has become so ingrained in the policy repertoire of an organization or a government.

2.5 Transparency

Although more a procedural idea than a substantive policy idea, transparency has been commonly advocated for improving government performance in dealing with a range of policy issues (see Erkkillä, 2012; Fung et al., 2007). Indeed, for some reformers transparency has been almost a panacea for all that ails government. The assumption has been that if politicians, government agencies and their members have to make decisions "in the sunshine,"[9] then they will be more likely to make decisions that the public will like. Further, they will be less likely to engage in corruption or misuse of their public positions. And some have even argued that knowing how decisions that affect them are made may be a basic human right (Birkinshaw, 2006).

While at a normative level transparency appears extremely desirable and democratic, in practical terms transparency can create real governance problems (Roberts, 2006). To some extent, the consequences of increased transparency are exactly the opposite of those intended by the policy – increased secrecy

---

[9] Some early versions of transparency laws in the United States were called "sunshine laws."

rather than increased openness. When faced with making difficult decisions, political and administrative leaders may not want to discuss the issues as a matter of public record, but instead will find private means of discussing them – phone calls, or a meeting at a coffee shop or on a park bench (Malesky et al., 2012). There will thus be no records of those discussions, whereas under rules demanding less transparency there might have been.

And for policies demanding high levels of transparency, difficult decisions may not be made at all, or decisions that are politically acceptable but suboptimal in policy terms may be adopted. Fritz Scharpf (1988) argued that these suboptimal decisions could result from multiple veto-players in a decision-making situation, but the same can result when the public functions as one large veto-player assessing the actions of their agents. Bargaining among decision-makers is likely to be constrained if their every position in a debate is made known to the public. But despite these issues, transparency continues to be offered as a cure for many things that ail public governance.

2.6 The Market is the Solution for Health Care Problems, Especially Cost

The assumption of the political Right in the United States – and somewhat also in other countries (Schut and Van de Ven, 2011; Homedes and Ugalde, 2005) – is that the solution for problems in health care, and especially health care costs, is greater competition and the creation of a more effective market for medical services. The diagnosis is that because of professional monopolies and the domination of large providers and large insurers, the health care market functions as an oligopoly and thus more competition would solve the observed problems of high costs and limited access. As in the neoclassical model, more providers would drive down the market-clearing price, and there would be more service and lower costs.

Although health care certainly does have some oligopolistic features, the fundamental assumption undergirding this policy idea – that health care is a market like all others – is perhaps the fundamental source of the enduring nature of this zombie idea.[10] This assumption has prevailed even though health care has few (if any) of the features of a competitive marketplace (but see Rosenthal, 2009). Entry into the market for providers is limited, for example.[11] Further, information is asymmetric and therefore genuine consumer choice is

---

[10] In the United States, to the extent that the Republican Party has developed an alternative to Obamacare, it is based on enhanced competition and consumer choice.

[11] Some extreme advocates of the market model have argued to change this, and to permit unlicensed practitioners and untested remedies to be available for patients. The assumption is that patients will learn who are the reliable providers and the others will be forced out of business

limited. The patient will have a difficult time ex ante knowing the quality, or even the safety, of the treatments he or she is being offered. Indeed, when consumers can choose, they often seek the highest price option, assuming that the quality of the treatment will be superior. And health care has some characteristics of a public good (e.g., for vaccinations), so simple market ideas will not be effective. Despite those problems, the idea of health as a market persists, as does the more general approach of privatization mentioned earlier.[12]

2.7 Prohibition as a Means of Addressing Substance Abuse

We mentioned the idea of prohibition earlier, when attempting to differentiate zombie ideas from other types of poor ideas. Most notably in the United States, there were attempts to eliminate the social and health problems caused by alcohol by preventing its sale or consumption (Schrad, 2010). This "noble experiment," so-called by Herbert Hoover, lasted slightly less than fourteen years, and did little to curb the use of alcohol in the United States. Although abandoned for alcohol, except for some remaining "dry" counties and municipalities in the United States, the same logic has been applied to the sale of "soft drugs" in much of the world, with varying penalties for the sale, use and possession of drugs such as marijuana.

Despite many attempts to legalize marijuana and cannabis, there are numerous jurisdictions – national, provincial and local – that maintain a policy of prohibition. Although the evidence may be subject to some sources of invalidity,[13] there appears to be small increases in consumption of marijuana along with corresponding reductions in alcohol consumption. There also has been some tendency toward a reduced number of traffic accidents and, in some cases, fewer incidences of violence (see Anderson and Rees, 2011). Further, as was true for the prohibition of alcohol, keeping soft drugs illegal makes them more expensive and hence encourages crime.

Like many other zombie ideas, prohibition is, on the face of it, very appealing, and may have a positive valence in Béland and Cox's (2013) terminology. Intuitively, it makes sense that if you want to prevent the consumption of alcohol or other intoxicants, then the simplest method is to ban the substance. Yet in this case, as in many others, intuition does not fare well when confronted with the complex chains of cause and effect that exist in the world of public

---

[12] In addition, Cashore and Nathan (2019) find that market-driven environmental policies in less developed countries may have perverse consequences for governance in those countries yet continue to be advocated and implemented.

[13] Reported use when marijuana has been legalized is higher than when it is illegal, for the obvious reason that respondents would be unwilling to report engaging in an illegal activity.

policy. But that intuition is why this idea and others that repeatedly fail do tend to persist.

2.8 The Military and Defense Ideas

The military have been a bountiful source of zombie ideas over the centuries. Generals are often accused of fighting the last war and using old ideas that are soon shown to be outmoded in changing circumstances and with changing technologies. The horrors of World War I have been attributed in part to the failure of generals to understand the capacity of the machine gun, and later the tank, to fundamentally alter the nature of war (Ellis, 1975). And later, the militaries in many countries were slow to abandon the lessons from World War I and to embrace newer technologies, notably the airplane (Hurley, 1975).

One of the dominant ideologies in the American defense establishment has been the capacity of air power – and especially strategic bombing – to substitute for "boots on the ground" in winning conflicts. This ideology developed during World War II and has been a standard tenet of the military establishment since that time. This has been true despite the absence of reliable evidence to support the idea. To some extent, the absence of reliable evidence has been the result of the strength of the belief in the theory and the failure to perform objective assessments (Gentile, 2001).

The use of analogies has been a particular means by which zombie (or at least suspect) ideas have survived in foreign policy. The most notable analogy for the past three-quarters of a century has been Munich and the dangers of appeasement (Houghton, 1996). Politicians in a number of countries, but especially the United States and the United Kingdom, have used, or been used by, this analogy to pursue military interventions when more diplomatic routes for resolving international conflicts might have been available. During the Cold War period, the "domino theory" was an important codicil to the appeasement argument (Hastings, 2018).

2.9 Local and State Solutions to National Problems

One generic policy idea that has come from both the Left and the Right is that it is possible to use solutions at a subnational level to address national policy problems. The two best examples, however, may come from the political Left, and from the United States. One of these is that it is possible to address gun violence adequately with state and local laws. Many liberal states and cities pass gun control laws of various sorts, and then see their efforts undermined by the movement of guns bought legally or illegally into the state (Kleck, 2012). These laws may make it somewhat more difficult for the would-be gun-owner and user, but there is no real control over the number of weapons within the state.

Another common attempt to use subnational policymaking when national level solutions appear impossible is for climate change, or environmental policy more generally. Again, liberal states or provinces may act in this policy domain by attempting to reduce pollution or CO_2 emissions within their territory, only to "import" emissions from neighboring jurisdictions, and perhaps the world at large. And, in the process, they risk losing employment as firms seek locations with less regulation This idea does not always fail, however. Perhaps the best example of this strategy working well is California's emission control requirements for automobiles. The market in California is sufficiently large that the state can influence the design of automobiles for the entire US market (Davenport and Tabuchi, 2019), and the state may therefore really have some broader influence.

This continuing utilization of subnational solutions to broader problems indicates a failure to take into account the *scale* of public sector problems (Schulman, 1980). That is, some public problems are inherently large-scale and can only be addressed at the national or even the international level (Levin et al., 2012). Attempts to do otherwise produce inadequate outcomes and may waste a great deal of time and money. Yet, the appeal, for citizens and for politicians, of producing local solutions perpetuates the use of this zombie policy idea.

Although we are emphasizing the use of policies at a subnational level to address national-level problems, this may be part of a general mismatch between the size of the domain and the territory in which the policy is being applied. We mentioned earlier that local governments may be used to address climate change issues when they could better be considered national. These problems could, however, also be considered international. The difficulty for policymakers is that there is no effective government at the international level for climate change – or, indeed, for many other important policy problems.[14]

2.10 Conceptual and Measurement Issues

Although the examples presented illustrate the concept of zombie ideas, we are still left with some definitional and conceptual questions. The most obvious is: How long does the idea have to persist in the face of evidence of failure before we can say it is a zombie? One way of addressing this question is to look at the

---

[14] This puts climate change into the category of "super-wicked problems," it having all the characteristics of a wicked problem as well as the absence of an effective governance mechanism (Levin et al., 2012).

number of times the idea has been adopted, even without any tangible success in achieving its stated goals. For example, the idea of tax cuts as a means of fostering economic growth has been implemented in most Republican administrations in the USA since at least the end of World War II, with relatively little success (see Table 1).

Another conceptual issue is: How do we know that a policy has failed, and hence are able to say that an idea persists in the face of failure? Few policies are complete failures, or complete successes, and failure is often in the eye of the beholder. Further, few policies have singular and unambiguous goals, and success on one dimension may be accompanied by failures on others. For example, the tax cuts passed in the Trump administration had modest effects on overall economic growth, but did succeed in boosting the stock market and in moving money to corporations and wealthy Republican donors (Hale et al., 2018).

A third conceptual issue is how to understand the role of context in the failure, and possible success, of policies. We can say that a policy has failed before and therefore assume that it will fail again, while its advocates can argue that the previous failure was the result of circumstances rather than the inherent validity of the policy. Thus, being able to make any definitive statements about the success or failure of policies, and the extent to which policy ideas may survive too long, involves being able to specify clearly the factors in the environment that contributed to the outcomes of the policy choice and discount their effects.[15]

The role of context in understanding success and failure is all the more important in an era that emphasizes evidence-based policymaking. If indeed evidence is to be transported from one setting to another and used to argue for the utility of a particular policy, then the context within which that evidence arose is crucial for understanding its relevance for another context (Behague et al., 2009). While the relevance of context is difficult to deny, identifying what it is about context, and about policy ideas, that matters for making a good match is not easy. The difficulties in making policy transfers generally occur when attempting to transfer ideas from affluent countries to less-affluent ones. But the absence of wealth is not the only factor inhibiting effective transfers, and policy transfers can be daunting even among seemingly similar countries.

The final conceptual question is: When is an idea the same idea? This is in some ways the classic Heraclitus problem of assessing change and stability. For example, the concepts of policy drift (Rocco and Thurston, 2014) and policy

---

[15] This can be conceptualized as a quasi-experimental research design. The researcher does not have any control over the occurrence of the contextual events but would have to discount their effects after the fact (see Campbell and Stanley, 1963).

conversion that were developed in historical institutionalism point to the continuing changes of policies. Earlier research has also pointed to the extent to which policymaking is often remaking existing policies rather than innovating (Carter, 2012). Can we say that these zombie policies that may adapt over time are really the same policy? And how much change is necessary to say that a new policy has indeed been created?

2.11 Summary

At the extreme, advocates on both the political Right and the political Left argue that many, if not most, of the policy ideas we currently follow are in the zombie category (see Judt, 2010). In environmental policy, Extinction Rebellion and climate change deniers both oppose contemporary environmental policies, albeit for very different reasons. And deficit hawks on one side and economic expansionists on the other both reject contemporary budgetary policies (see Blyth, 2013). In this Element we are adopting a less extreme position on the viability of existing policy regimes, but there are still many ideas in effect, and being advocated, that appear to be surviving after their utility has been exhausted – assuming they had any utility in the first instance.

The beauty of policy ideas, however, remains in the eye of the beholder. Although we argue from as objective a position as we can muster that the policy ideas mentioned herein are of dubious value, many people actively involved in the policy process will continue to advocate them. All of the zombie policies discussed here continue to have strong advocates, continue to appear in active policy discussions, and continue to be adopted and then implemented. This persistence of zombie ideas may represent, as in Samuel Johnson's description of second marriages, the triumph of hope over experience, but perhaps more than hope, there often is sincere conviction.

3 Why Do Zombie Ideas Persist?

With some idea of the nature of policy ideas that persist in the face of evidence – strong evidence, in some cases – that they are not valid, we now proceed to consider why these ideas do survive. There is no single reason, and we cannot necessarily relate any particular reason for persistence to a particular failed policy idea. Several scholars in policy studies and related fields have also wondered about the ability of poor ideas to survive and even to thrive. For example, Jeffrey Pfeffer (2005) has considered why poor ideas, especially those based on economics, persist in management. And many scholars of foreign and defense policy have lamented the continuing use of ideas such as the domino theory (see Hastings, 2018). Some of the explanations offered for these cases of persistence are idiosyncratic and are based on particular characteristics of their policy domain, but we will attempt to develop more general explanations.

Much of the discussion of the persistence of policy ideas revolves around the role of institutions and organizations in preserving these ideas as a "logic of appropriateness" (March and Olsen, 2011) for their actions. This explanation may anthropomorphize organizations; it does, however, point to the importance of mission statements (Goodsell, 2011) and other organizational ideologies in shaping policy. Organizations and institutions use those ideas to socialize their new members, and also use them in their political battles with other organizations and with their sponsors over budgets, policy and survival (March, 1996).

3.1 Types of Explanation

What will follow is something of a "shopping list" of possible explanations for the persistence of zombie ideas, but those specific explanations can be classified into several large categories. At the end of the aforementioned shopping list we will develop, in the form of several tables, a number of hypotheses about the ways in which these general types of explanation are linked to the specific. These hypotheses are, of course, preliminary and perhaps extremely difficult to test in any definitive manner, but they may be a means of structuring further research on the survival of ideas (bad and good) in public policymaking.

1) Elites. The first level at which zombie ideas gain some sustenance is from elites. These elites are primarily political, but they can also be policy experts who have commitments to certain ideas. In some ways, experts may be a more significant source of zombie ideas than politicians, in part because experts tend to propose the policy ideas that are then adopted by politicians. But that expertise can also lead to hubris and a failure to consider alternatives to the conventional advice that has been and continues to be given. The policy experts who continue to advocate ideas to which they are committed but which have proven ineffective thus help perpetuate zombie ideas.

As Berger and Luckman (1966) point out, there is a social distribution of knowledge, and a failure to consider sources other than experts may produce failure, and continuing failure, in policymaking (Koppl, 2018). With the development of the Internet and the greater democratization of knowledge about policy, the dominance of elites in utilizing knowledge in policy has been diminished. But what may have been emerging is an inability to assess information independently and to make choices about the reliability of data. Each set of policy ideas may now have its own set of "facts" without a judge for the correctness of the information being used. In an age without agreed standards of truth of ideas or information, zombie ideas will find fertile ground.

But political elites usually cannot be absolved of blame for continuing policy failures from poor ideas. They choose those experts who will support their political preferences, and use those preferences when making policy choices. They create the demand for policy ideas, zombie or otherwise. And, having latched on to an idea that has been successful politically (if not substantively) in the past, they are likely to continue to use that idea. Political parties often exhibit some of the features of Groupthink (see Section 3.2.2; for a lament, see Dodson, 2019), so elections may be the major remedy for the persistence of elite ideas.

Elections may provide for some competition among ideas to find the best and to weed out the worst – including the zombies – but this mechanism assumes that the ordinary citizen is adequately equipped to sort through potentially complex policy ideas and identify the best and, more importantly, reject the worst.[16] The danger is that ordinary citizens may be as wedded, or more wedded, to zombie ideas than are the elites. Political elites may use these tired old ideas as means of winning elections, but the average member of the public may not have thought very deeply about policy ideas and the options for moving away from the familiar when making policy.[17]

The arguments presented here about the behavior of elites when making decisions to maintain zombie ideas tend to assume rather conservative behavior on their part. The argument is that political and administrative decision-makers, when confronted with choosing a familiar idea (even if flawed) or a more innovative idea, will opt for the familiar. This argument tends to conflict with the argument of prospect theory (see Bellé, Cantarelli and Belardinelli, 2018), which argues that when decision-makers are faced with risk and the possibility of loss, they choose riskier solutions that may promise greater returns (see also Weyland, 2008).

The choices of ideas and strategies being made may, however, depend on the perceptions of the decision that must be made, with policymaking being perhaps significantly different from other types of decision-making. Further, these decisions are not made in a vacuum, and blame avoidance (see Section 3.2.7) is a well-established routine in political life that may lead political leaders to make conservative decisions even when faced with possible losses. And, finally, prospect theory also points to the importance of a status quo bias in decision-

---

[16] This weeding out of poor ideas is difficult given that elections may be about a number of different policy areas and a number of contending policy ideas. The ordinary citizen may not be well equipped to cope with the number and complexity of issues and may therefore focus on a limited number of familiar issues.

[17] Some zombie ideas for policymaking may make a great deal of sense to the ordinary citizen and will resonate with their experiences. For example, the analogy between the public budget and the household budget may appear sensible to the individual who must balance their own budget every month.

making (Moynihan and Lavertu, 2012), with the zombie idea being very much the status quo in the policy domain, and therefore, despite any risk calculation, perhaps the preferred solution to the problem.

2) Organizational. Most policy elites, whether political or administrative, do not function alone but are members of organizations, and most of those organizations will have their own commitments to policy ideas. These ideas may be the familiar standard operating procedures of organizations, or may represent Allison and Zelikow's (1999) organizational process model of decision-making. Organizations develop routines in responding to issues in their policy domains and most of those routines have some justification through policy ideas (Bach and Weigrich, 2019). These routines can, of course, be justified through zombie ideas just as easily as through more successful policy approaches. Further, those zombie ideas may be used to rationalize organizational self-interests and are used to promote the organization's position in policy and budget skirmishes with other organizations.[18] These ideas may be as well-known outside the organization as within, and that familiarity can be useful in justifying the policy.

Organizations are, of course, composed of individuals, and we should not anthropomorphize them excessively, but organizations may replicate their ideas and their biases as they socialize new members and pass along the policy commitments of the organization. The normative version of institutionalism (March and Olsen, 1989) emphasizes the extent to which organizational and institutional socialization tend to perpetuate ideas, good or bad, that are the foundations for the "logic of appropriateness" within the institution. In addition, individuals may be "pre-socialized" and choose to work for a particular public sector organization because of its values and policies – environmentalists will want to join the Ministry of the Environment, for example.

Organizations may have preferences not only for specific policies, but also for specific policy instruments. Previous research (Linder and Peters, 1989) has demonstrated that organizations and institutions have preferred instruments and tend to use them whenever faced with a policymaking challenge. These solutions may be inappropriate for the new policy problem being confronted, but the organization will persist in adopting that instrument. This persistence is in part simple path dependence, but it is also a recognition that the organization will better understand how to implement this instrument than it would any

---

[18] When used consciously to promote organizational self-interest, the ideas come closer to Allison's bureaucratic politics model. Indeed, the use of ideas – zombie and otherwise – was evident in his analysis of the Cuban missile crisis (Allison and Zelikow, 1999).

alternatives, and hence may it be a superior administrative choice whilst not necessarily the best policy choice.

3) Society/Individual. Finally, zombie ideas are likely to die a final death if there is no popular support for them. This proposition is obviously true in a democratic regime, but over time may also be true in nondemocratic regimes. If elites who are using zombie ideas for electoral purposes, or for purposes of political mobilization, do not find a receptive audience, then those ideas will wither away. This withering away may take some time – there are still some political elites who would like to return to the gold standard – but without the capacity of the ideas to find support in society they would have little impact on policy.

The role of society in the preservation of zombie ideas should not be underestimated. If members of the society are not receptive to the policy ideas that are being advanced, then those ideas are unlikely to survive. The political elites will not be passive and can engage in information or propaganda campaigns to advance certain ideas, but if not successful in inculcating the idea into the minds of the public they are unlikely to successful in advancing the policy. Obviously, this need for at least some popular support is more important for democratic regimes, but may also be important even in less democratic regimes (see Tang, 2016).

In addition, society is composed of interests, whether organized or not. As we argued earlier, economic and social interests may be unwilling to express blatant self-interest, so they will therefore need to dress up those interests with ideas; tax cuts are argued not just on the basis that they will benefit the wealthy, but also that they will promote economic growth that will benefit everyone. These interests will need to work through political elites in order to have the influence on policy that they want, but having these ideas to support their efforts will make the task easier. And the ideas will be important in democratic regimes for generating political support for the policies.

4) Summary. These three levels of explanation for the persistence of ideas, whether good or bad, can be treated separately, but they are also closely connected. Government elites are inevitably influenced by their own society, and they also understand the limitations placed on their policy choices by that society. And those political elites also work within organizations, influencing, and being influenced by, those organizations. Disentangling these interactions presents difficult research challenges and may also represent different theoretical casts of minds. Much of contemporary political science focuses on the role of individual preferences, but the institutionalist logic assumes that those preferences are shaped by organization memberships rather than being exogenous and fixed.

3.2 Explanations for the Survival of Ideas

As well as utilizing the three basic types of explanation for the survival of policy ideas in the face of substantive failure, we should also examine some more specific reasons for survival. These more specific explanations for the survival of ideas can be related to the more basic varieties, but understanding the dynamics involved in the individual explanations can generate hypotheses that can be tested with reference to the survival of individual zombie ideas. While there are methodological issues involved in testing these hypotheses, as we have already discussed, they can be used to develop our thinking about the linkage of policy ideas, the persistence of ideas, and perhaps even the adoption of new policies.

We should also point out that some of the same logic that is being used to explain the persistence of zombie ideas can be used to explain the persistence of more effective policy ideas. Policy ideas – good, bad and indifferent – are always contending in a marketplace of ideas. Good (here meaning successful) policy ideas may not survive just because they are successful. They will continue to be challenged by other ideas and need strategies and resources in order to survive. The explanations we provide for the survival of zombie ideas may not be as crucial for better approaches to policy, but they can still be important.

The explanations offered herein for the survival of zombie ideas are political and social. We should also recognize that some ideas, whether they are likely to produce policy success or not, are simply more appealing to the public, and to leaders, than are others. Béland and Cox (2013) discuss this emotional appeal in terms of the "valence" of an idea, using the example of sustainability as an idea that was very appealing to many target populations. The emotional appeal of ideas can be used by policy advocates to build coalitions for policies and programs, regardless of the more cognitive dimension of success or failure.[19] And policy ideas with a positive valence have a greater probability of becoming "policy paradigms" and influencing policy choices across time and across countries (Hall, 1993).

3.2.1 Simple Path Dependence

The simplest explanation for the persistence of ideas is the logic of path dependence, now associated with historical institutionalism (Sydow,

---

[19] The idea of valence can be linked to the use of symbols, discussed in Section 3.2.3.

Schreyögg and Koch, 2009). The logic is that, once created, an institution will tend to persist until it is replaced by another, usually through a rather extreme punctuation. Later versions of change within historical institutionalism (Maloney and Thelen, 2010) have identified less dramatic forms of change, in which the institutions – or, in our case, ideas[20] – would be transformed while still retaining some elements of the original idea. Or, alternatively, a policy domain may be characterized by several layers of ideas, with older ideas that are perhaps no longer viable continuing to have some influence despite the presence of newer policy concepts.

The path dependence argument is especially important for understanding policy ideas that have been successful at some point in their history but later began to fail. That failure may be the result of changing politics, or, more likely, changing socioeconomic conditions, but a policy idea simply becomes out-moded. But if we adopt Pierson's (2000) arguments about path dependence for institutions, some actors in the policy process will have been receiving positive feedbacks from the idea and will continue to utilize it until sufficient evidence, or political power, accumulates to alter their behavior. For example, agricultural subsidies in Europe have been criticized for years as being outmoded, but continue to be dispensed because both political elites and agricultural interests receive positive feedbacks from them.

Mark Blyth (2001) has discussed path dependency explicitly in terms of ideas, rather than institutions, and describes policy ideas as being "locked" into a policymaking system to the exclusion of others. Whereas most versions of historical institutionalism focus on institutions or physical products, Blyth's argument focuses on ideas and the role that they play in placing a mortmain on the consideration of alternatives, including those that may be superior to the idea being implemented. And, unlike in Pierson's argument, self-interest of the participants is not necessarily a factor in the persistence of the idea.

Path dependence of zombie ideas may also be important because of the coordinative effects of these policies. That is, any one policy – based on a zombie idea or not – does not exist in a vacuum. It is embedded in a policy and institutional field, and the other actors in that field will have expectations about what policies will be implemented. Just as institutions may become isomorphic because of their interactions with other institutions (Dimaggio and Powell, 1991), so too can policies become similar to those with which they interact. Public sector agencies have experience with certain types of policy and can adapt their own programs more easily to programs that they know and

---

[20] Although phrased in institutional terms, historical institutionalism was to a great extent based on ideas. The structures responsible for delivering a policy are tangible, but they are formed on the basis of less tangible ideas. See, for example, Hall (1989).

understand – even if they are not the best policies. Thus, maintaining path dependence of policies is important within this broader policy arena.

In addition, as Sarigil (2015) argues, policies often become habits and are adopted and perpetuated with very little conscious thought. Once a policy response to a problem becomes habitual, there may be little reason, or even opportunity, to consider alternative policies. That said, the behaviors associated with habits are not entirely mechanical, and also have meaning for the actor who is acting out of habit. In the case of policy ideas – again, zombie or not – this may mean that the actor has internalized those values and they are not an automatic response; rather, they are perceived to be the proper and legitimate policy choice.

The several incremental forms of change now associated with historical institutionalism and path dependence can also help us to understand why zombie ideas persist (Mahoney and Thelen, 2010). For example, layering as a means of change can be used to embed an old idea within the organization's operating routines, where it may be influential even if other, newer ideas are layered on top. Likewise, with conversion, an old policy idea may be retained but be used differently to justify policy choices. For example, in changing welfare states, social-democratic ideas about justice and equality may be used to justify the equality of a marketplace rather than equality before the law.

3.2.2 Beliefs and Ideology

Second, as already noted, policy ideas are based on beliefs. Those may be simple beliefs about the efficacy of a particular approach to public policy, or they may be broader, ideological belief patterns. In either case, the policymaker is making his or her choices based on beliefs that may be justified more by faith than by evidence. In addition to the general difficulties imposed by the power of beliefs on policy, we also need to recognize that many of these beliefs have poor, or virtually nonexistent, micro-assumptions. That is, many of the zombie ideas mentioned herein are supported by firm beliefs but little else. For example, the famous Laffer Curve has been investigated by economists from conservative think tanks and appears to work only, if at all, under severely constrained and somewhat unusual circumstances. Likewise, the motivational effects of work requirements appear weak, so the success of the programs may be simply in saving money because potential clients are excluded.

Persistent patterns of belief may be individual but, as noted, organizations also play a major role in the persistence of ideas. Groupthink has been identified as the tendency of small groups not to challenge the conventional wisdom within the group (Janis, 1991). This can be seen as a manifestation of the power of collective beliefs over policy. This approach to understanding deci-sion-making argues that groups develop internal beliefs that they use to justify their actions and to maintain internal cohesion within the group. While the principal interest of Janis was in the group dynamics involved, ideas are important elements and the availability of a set of agreed-upon ideas is import-ant for the ease of creating concurrence within the group (see 't Hart, 1990).

The positive reinforcement in path dependence mentioned above may also be a function of beliefs rather than more substantive feedbacks such as organiza-tional or personal success. The use of a familiar idea to justify a policy may make the individual involved "feel good" when his or her views are validated within the group, or by the policy choices of that group and other elites. And, from an organizational perspective, this also supports the existing organization given that its current standard responses to policy problems are confirmed and therefore their budget can be maintained or even expanded.

Identifying the importance of ideologies in the persistence of zombie ideas leads us to think about one of the major "ghost" ideas that has never been adopted seriously, in the United States at least – gun control. The dynamic here is very much the same as the role of ideologies in the perpetuation of zombie ideas that exist in practice. Despite overwhelming international evidence, gun control is opposed not only on constitutional grounds but also on practical grounds (Jacobs, 2002). Both of those arguments against gun control depend heavily on beliefs and particular interpretations of the evidence, and the rejec-tion of other forms of evidence.

3.2.3 Symbolism

The symbolic values of zombie ideas are closely related to the role of beliefs and ideology. We will focus on the capacity of zombie ideas to have symbolic impacts in the broader society, as well as with the individuals who hold the causal beliefs. Policymakers may be interested in satisfying members of their own political group, but they also have to appeal to citizens as a whole if they are to be successful politically. Therefore, policy ideas that have symbolic appeal among that broader population will be more likely to persist than will policy ideas that appeal primarily to policy elites.

Zombie ideas, as is true for other items seeking a place on the political agenda, must have some linkage to political and social symbols. With those symbolic linkages in place, the advocates of the policy will have more success in getting the issue onto the agenda and having it adopted by government. Take, for example, the tax cut policies that continue to be recycled in the United States and elsewhere. These are linked closely to symbols such as the "free market" and the liberty of the individual to make his or her choices about how to spend the money they earn. The presumed linkage to economic growth is important, but the symbolic element provides a first step in having these policies adopted again and again. These policy ideas have "halo effects" (Krugman, 2020), such that one idea is linked to a broader ideology of the role of the state in society.

These familiar political and economic symbols may be used to create false analogies that can be useful for maintaining ineffective policies. For example, advocates of balanced budgets at the national level will invoke the picture of a couple sitting at their kitchen table attempting to pay all their bills and to make their income match their expenditures. The family budget is a familiar challenge to many citizens: the proposition is then advanced that the national budget should be no different, and therefore the country should return to pre-Keynesian economic policies. While in many ways maintaining a balanced national budget may be desirable, in many instances deficits are also desirable as fiscal policy interventions. The symbols and the analogies are useful means for justifying the older, and largely outdated, policies.

3.2.4 Politics and Power

For political scientists, perhaps the first explanation that might come to mind for why poor ideas would persist in policymaking is politics and power. Ideas are a means of justifying self-interest, and of clothing political power in a more acceptable garb (see Hay, 2011). In Blyth's (2001) terms they are weapons. Just as the individual's self-interest may be relatively stable, so too may the ideas that are employed to justify it politically. Therefore, unless there is some significant evidence to refute the existing patterns of belief and practice, the old ideas will continue.

The zombie ideas that are being used to maintain and enhance political power cannot stand on their own. They must, as already noted, have an audience that accepts at least some of the logic of the ideas. For example, the various market-based ideas mentioned earlier that have been capable of surviving past their normal life span have done so because a significant portion of the population in the United States believes in free market economics, albeit in a somewhat unstudied manner. In particular, the analogy between the economy of the household and that of a nation state has tended to pervade popular thinking about fiscal policy. If it is not good for an individual to owe thousands of dollars, then certainly it must be awful for a country to owe trillions.[21]

---

[21] There is, of course, J. Paul Getty's adage that if you the bank $100, that's your problem; if you owe the bank $100 million, that's the bank's problem.

When we follow the core idea of elitism, there is an ongoing debate about the source of power. It might stem from an economic or social base, or because an elite has occupied major positions in the military force or in political offices. Winters and Page (2009), for instance, argue that the American political economy is both an oligarchy and a democracy. In this context, oligarchy is understood as the politics of wealth defense. The authors introduce the Material Power Index and show how money can be translated into political power. Accountants, lawyers and wealth management consultants form magic circles, which leads to unequal influence in the hands of a small group. An elitist would argue that zombie ideas prevail because they serve the interest of the few, who, on the one hand, are capable of defending their own policies and, on the other hand, are sufficiently rich and powerful to kill conflictual policies.

Two structural features of political regimes may also influence the preservation of ideas that may have outlived their utility. One is the consensual nature of politics, as identified by Arend Lijphart (2012), in many European systems. As the name implies, a consensual political system has some basic agreement among the parties and major actors about the course of public policy. In contrast to majoritarian systems, in which there is some alternation of policy ideas, the consensual system will facilitate the maintenance of policy paths once established. These consensual systems have, however, come under attack in recent decades as an increase in populist mobilization has questioned the underlying assumptions and policy ideas being implemented (Schumacher and Van Kersbergen, 2016).

Corporatism is a second structural feature of government with a potential impact on zombie ideas. In corporatist systems, privileged groups (organized labor and capital) gain access to government decision-makers (Schmitter, 1974). They become incorporated into the state and are supposed to guarantee a risk-free policy implementation (Gill, 2014) while demolishing political conflicts. The privileged access of labor and capital to political decision-making serves as an explanation for why certain policy ideas prevail.

And, finally, even in the absence of consensual or corporatist politics, a policy idea or policy paradigm may be used to form and maintain a political coalition. Zombie ideas from the political Left are used to create coalitions among Left parties, and the same is true for parties on the Right. The major political tendencies may have internal differences, but they may share a number of causal beliefs that they can use to cement coalitions. Those causal beliefs do not have to be accurate so long as they are believed by the participants within the coalition and can be used to create sufficient agreement to form a viable coalition.

The above arguments emphasize the role of consensus and continuity in the preservation of largely defunct policy ideas. Paul Krugman (2020) makes a contradictory argument, emphasizing the role of division and politicization in maintaining poor policy ideas. His analysis of contemporary American politics is that the extreme divisions between Right and Left have made it possible for comfortable ideas within each camp to persist unchallenged. Further, each of the warring tribes develops its own facts as well as its own ideas, so that again there is no effective challenge to the persistence of failed programs and policies.

3.2.5 Policy Entrepreneurship

Policy entrepreneurs have been recognized as important actors in moving policies through the policymaking process (Mintrom and Luetjens, 2017). These policy entrepreneurs have usually been discussed as a source of policy innovation (see Kingdon, 2003), and are assumed to be developing new ideas in the anticipation of the opening of "policy windows." The entrepreneur is then ready with an idea to take through that window of opportunity and to make new policy. Policy entrepreneurs have been assumed to be a major source of change in public policy, and as innovators in policy process (Mintrom and Norman, 2009).

The policy entrepreneur may also be selling outdated and unsuccessful ideas as well as policy innovations. Committed to a set of policy ideas, an entrepreneur may survive inside or outside of government, waiting for the opportunity to reintroduce those ideas just as a more innovative entrepreneur may be waiting for an opening for a new idea. Political leaders coming into office often want ideas and policy guidance, and the entrepreneur is ready and able to supply it, whether the ideas are new and innovative or old and shopworn. And if the policy entrepreneurs are existing members of public organizations, they may be more likely to be proffering older ideas.

Policy entrepreneurs may be committed to complete policies, meaning a definition of the problem as well as the modes of intervention, but they may also be committed to policy instruments. This may be because of their personal beliefs in the efficacy of the instrument, or it may be because their organization is specialized in the application of this instrument and adopting the instrument may mean also supporting the budget and prestige of the organization (see Béland and Howlett, 2016). For example, social policy organizations may be very adept at running social insurance programs and may advocate them even when the problem being addressed, (e.g., medical care for the elderly) is not well-suited for the instrument. The Medicare program in the United States, for example, was designed in this manner (Davis and Schoen, 1978).

3.2.6 Links to Individuals

The links of a policy to powerful symbols, and the role of individuals as policy entrepreneurs, can be important for maintaining zombie ideas, but those two may be to some extent combined, and at times old and ineffective policies may be maintained simply by links with individuals. These individuals most commonly are political leaders who have a coterie of supporters who accept their ideas with little question and may continue to defend, and implement, those ideas after the individual has left office. The individuals may also be policy thinkers whose ideas become accepted as dogma and may be unquestioned even when they prove to be outdated.

The coronavirus pandemic, as is true for any major crisis, has tended to compress policy time and space. A policy may become old quickly as more information becomes available and new remedies are considered. That means that an idea may become a zombie within weeks. For example, without any scientific backing, President Trump touted the use of hydroxychloroquine, a drug used to treat malaria and lupus, as a cure for COVID-19. However, even after another drug – remdesivir – appeared and had scientific support for its efficacy in treating the virus, many (if not most) of Trump's supporters continued to advocate the unproved remedy simply because it had initially been advocated by the president (Nguyen, 2020).

The same commitments to individuals may occur over longer time spans. The connection of individuals to policies, and especially zombie policies, may be most apparent in authoritarian countries where the leader can do no wrong. One of the more egregious examples was the "Great Leap Forward" in China that caused millions of deaths from famine, while officials were unwilling to report the devastation resulting from this economic plan to Chairman Mao (Li and Tao Yang, 2005). Again, compared to the persistence of ideas with the Kim regime in North Korea, this was a short period, but the mistakes continued to be repeated year after year.

3.2.7 Blame Avoidance

It has been argued that policymaking, and governance more generally, is about claiming credit and avoiding blame (Weaver, 1986; Hood, 2011). That is, political leaders (and public organizations) who can plausibly take credit for positive outcomes and can avoid being connected with negative outcomes are likely to be successful, all else being equal. Given that we are focusing attention on the role of failed policy ideas in government, the possibilities for claiming credit appear limited, but that only makes blame avoidance more important.

Choosing a policy that has failed previously might appear an unlikely way to avoid blame, but in practice it may not be. If the policy being chosen has been tried before, it has to some extent been included in the (notional) list of approved policies for governments.[22] Therefore, choosing such a policy is less dangerous politically than choosing an innovative policy. Such an innovation, if unsuccessful, would clearly be labeled as being the policy of that political leader. Choosing an established form of intervention, even if not successful in the past, is following in familiar footsteps and hence is less dangerous.

Wolfgang Seibel (1992) coined the term "functional dilettantism" to explain relationships between the third sector and local governments. Local governments are fully aware that third sector organizations are likely to fail when they implement certain policies. Moreover, they assume that they (the local government) would also fail. However, third sector organization's dilettantism is functional for the maintenance of the local government's image. Local governments avoid the blame and let third sector organizations fail.

Blame avoidance through the adoption of familiar (if faulty) policies can also be connected with the use of analogies in justifying policy ideas and policy choices. If a policy can be made to look like an old policy, even if it is itself newer, it is likely to be more palatable and to generate less blame. For example, the appeal of "Medicare for All" in the United States was due at least in part to the fact that it was made to seem just more Medicare, rather than what was in reality a national health insurance program. In this case, Medicare is a less than perfect health insurance program, but it is not really a zombie. Yet advocating this program may forestall the search for a better single-payer plan for the entire population

3.2.8 Filtering Information and Ideas

The world of policymaking is complex and contains a great deal of information and numerous ideas. Likewise, there is no shortage of ideas about policy, and no shortage of policy entrepreneurs willing to "sell" those ideas. The problem is that some of those entrepreneurs are really hucksters, selling poor or disproved ideas to an unsuspecting set of potential clients/policymakers. On the face of it, discerning the gold of policy ideas from the dross is difficult. The hucksters may come from seemingly respectable organizations and have proper academic qualifications, but the "evidence" they are selling for evidence-based policy is weak or faulty (see, for example, Sherman, 2003).

Therefore organizations (and individuals) responsible for making policies need to exercise some filtering to minimize the negative effects of the "blooming, buzzing confusion of the world (James, 1890, 488)." Thus, we encounter one of the paradoxes of policymaking. While bounded rationality

---

[22] This could analogous to the "institutional agenda" of governments in agenda research. See Cobb and Elder (1971).

(Jones, 1999) and the associated filtering devices for removing many alternatives from consideration is crucial for minimizing decision-making costs in the public sector, it can also be a source of error, and of the persistence of zombie ideas. In this perspective, the rational organization places limits on the range of ideas and information considered when making a decision and, in the process, may perpetuate poor solutions simply because better solutions are considered to take too much time to evaluate, or are too far from the status quo.

But information may also be overly filtered, especially within organizations that have a commitment to a particular set of policy ideas. The excessive filtering of information and ideas can also be manifested in the isolation of decision-makers from the realities of their policy domains as they function "on the ground" (Thompson, 1977). One standard critique of organizations, whether public or private, is that the information held by the lower levels of the organization do not make it to the top and therefore poor policies will persist. That filtering, whether intentional or not, may privilege the ideas on which organizational policies are built, rather than newer alternatives.

We should also remember that political institutions may not provide the type of filtering of policy ideas that would be desirable if zombie ideas are finally to be killed off. This absence of institutional filtering is especially important when the zombie ideas are resident within the public bureaucracy, and the obvious source of filtering is the political class leading government. Unfortunately, far too few of those political leaders have the knowledge and experience necessary to perform the task of assessing policy ideas adequately.

Leaving aside the more egregious cases such as Donald Trump, many political leaders lack substantive knowledge concerning the policy domains for which they are responsible. Richard Rose (1976) pointed out that ministers coming into office rarely had any training or experience in their policy domain. That absence of any formal background in the policy domain is complicated by the relatively short time spans many ministers spend in one office, due to cabinet shuffles and coalition changes (Riddell, 2019). These problems of inadequate policy knowledge are perhaps most apparent in the Westminster governments, with ministers having to be members of parliament, but are certainly not unheard of elsewhere.

Therefore, the politicians who should be expected to do the filtering of policy ideas being "pitched" to them may be very poorly prepared for that task. Even if they are supported by advisors and a personal staff, they may still have to make sense of multiple policy ideas and then make a decision. As we have argued throughout this Element, when confronted with old ideas and new ideas, many individuals – whether politicians or not – may be more comfortable sticking with the old ideas and not taking the risk of pushing for new ideas. This may be true whether the ideas have been proven effective or not – they are still familiar.

Democratic political systems should, despite the faults identified by Rose and others, be better at filtering information and utilizing knowledge than nondemocratic systems. The competition within democratic politics can be a contest of ideas, and therefore should be able to eliminate zombie ideas. But not all democracies are equal in their abilities to eliminate poor policy ideas. Although scholars such as Arend Lijphart (2012) have praised consensual democracies for their stability, they may not perform the filtering function as well as majoritarian systems (see Shapiro, 2017; Rosenbluth and Shapiro, 2018). By fostering consensus and broad policy agreement, consensual systems may help sustain zombie ideas.

We could also argue the contrary position, however, concerning the relationship between the type of democratic system and the winnowing of zombie ideas. Consensual political systems will have more small parties that might take extreme positions. The dominant parties in these systems – both from the Right and from the Left – will maintain more common ideas and may be able to counter those more extreme ideas, even if the smaller radical parties gain representation in parliament. In majoritarian systems, if those more extreme ideas are adopted in one of the major parties, they may be able to persist, even if they are implemented only intermittently once the one party carrying that idea is in office. The "Stop-Go" economic policies of the United Kingdom in the 1960s and 1970s is a good example of such a pattern.

3.2.9 Biases–Disciplinary and Other

Following on from the interest in filtering information and ideas, another source of the perpetuation of poor policy ideas is disciplinary bias. This has been most noticeable in the inroads that economic reasoning has made in many policy domains, as well as in many other social science disciplines themselves. For example, Pfeffer (2005) argues that the adoption of economic concepts has significantly impacted management sciences, both public and private, and not positively. And this misplaced use of economic reasoning has, of course, been one of the standard critiques of New Public Management in public administration. The assumption with an ingrained disciplinary bias is that the discipline provides answers to a wide range of problems and hence can be used to address problems for which it may in reality be unsuited

Although it is easy to focus on biases held by academic disciplines, and the blinders they provide their adherents (Innes and Booher, 2018; see also Linder and Peters, 1989), the opposite can also be problematic for policy. That is, the failure of political elites to utilize expertise may help perpetuate the persistence of poor policy ideas as much as, or more than, clinging to a single disciplinary truth about the possible solutions for policy problems. Much of this resistance to academic expertise comes from the rejection of the utility of "theory" about policy (Walt, 2005). Rather than listen to any alternative approaches, policy-makers may be happy to persist in their own well-worn paths of policymaking, albeit suboptimal at best.

The biases that exist among disciplines and between academe and the world of practice represent additional important examples of the social division of knowledge (Berger and Luckmann, 1966) that may foster zombie ideas. No discipline has a monopoly on useful information and ideas, nor do academics (as much as we would like to believe it) have the answers for the world's problems. Likewise, practitioners, for all their experience in making policy, may not possess the understanding of policy required to produce change.

But managing an open and unbiased policy process is difficult, given the tendency of policymakers to seek closure and work "downstream" rather than "upstream" when considering problems.[23] Further, the availability of a solution may shape the definition of the problem being solved. The garbage can model, and other studies of multiple-stream policymaking, have demonstrated that solutions chase problems, and shape problems, as much as problems chase solutions. The development of more open and participatory policy design scenarios might be able to reduce the repetition of zombie ideas, or at least present some challenges to them.

Finally, there may also be geographical biases as well in how policy ideas are considered and adopted. We are presumed to live in a world of "evidence-based policymaking," where policymakers will scan the world for the best solutions to policy problems (Cairney, 2016). But there may be biases in the way in which those seeking solutions scan the available solutions. Those in the Anglo-American world may find solutions from within that group of nations more palatable, while Continental Europeans may stay within their own territory when looking for answers. Even within the United States, policymakers in northern states may not look south for answers, even with some southern states such as Mississippi having made major advances in policies such as education (Green and Goldstein, 2019).

---

[23] That is, they seek to find an answer quickly rather than considering a full range of solutions to the degree possible. This concept about decision-making comes from the policy design literature, especially the so-called "new design" (Bason, 2016; Peters, 2018), which tends to emphasize the development of a full complement of alternatives before coming to a conclusion about which solution may be best.

Bounded rationality argues that it is rational when confronted with a problem to engage in limited search behavior, considering primarily the options relatively near to the status quo (see Cyert and March, 1963). This strategy may well be viable if one is seeking to minimize decision-making costs, but it may also contribute to the perpetuation of zombie ideas. If a policy idea is flawed and is not working, then perhaps no amount of tinkering with it will ever produce a successful policy. Eliminating the zombie idea will require a more comprehensive search for policy alternatives, perhaps outside the usual comfort zone of the policymakers, and outside the biases that have supported the idea.

Biases in decision-making can also be related to the arguments from prospect theory (mentioned earlier). As well as the fundamental biases in decision-making related to risk-taking, there may also be a strong status quo bias in decision-making, for ordinary citizens as well as for the public sector. The known is very comfortable, and movement away from that familiar territory is uncomfortable. Therefore, decision-makers may well act on their biases in favor of status quo ideas, and citizens may applaud that unwillingness to think in more innovative ways.

3.2.10 Absence of Alternatives

Failed policy ideas also may persist simply because there is no available alternative. Governments are frequently in the position of having to respond to policy problems when they lack the capacity – intellectual or physical – to do so effectively. In the case of policy ideas for addressing these problems, governments will simply have to go back to what they have done in the past, even if it were not very effective. At least with a well-known policy option the consequences of the actions may be more predictable (but see Section 3.2.1). It may be better to able to anticipate the type of failure rather than cope with unknown, and potentially worse, failures. This cause for the persistence of zombie ideas is not entirely different from the idea of policy traps mentioned earlier (McConnell, 2019), although we are more concerned with the persistence of old ideas than the adoption of new ones.

Even when not operating in extremis, governments may still continue to implement a poor program simply because there is no other readily available option. Our discussion of the role of paradigms (see Section 1) argued that faulty paradigms will persist unless a superior alternative is available. In this case, "available" may mean either that the alternative has not yet been developed, or perhaps that there are no alternatives that are considered politically desirable or technically feasible. It may be perceived by a sitting government that it is better to perpetuate a familiar and enduring poor policy than to embark on a new course that has a significant chance of failure itself. Avoiding blame may be easier when using an established policy than when attempting to implement an innovative policy, and governments may eschew the opportunity to generate new solutions rather than pursue them.

The best example of the absence of alternatives in contemporary policy may be Obamacare (the Affordable Care Act) in the United States. From a design perspective, Obamacare is not a good program. It has too many moving parts; it depends upon too many actors in the public and private sectors – including citizens – doing what the program designers want; and it does not address many crucial health care problems, such as high drug costs. But the Republicans, in and out of Congress, have not been able to develop a credible alternative, so the program persists and has gained grudging support from a slight majority of Americans. Even as the courts chip away at the program, there is no alternative from the critics.

While there may in reality be no alternative policies at hand, the absence of alternatives may be politically constructed (Séville, 2017). Prime Minister Margaret Thatcher became famous for her "TINA" (There is no alternative) statements about policy and used this approach to quell discussions about the course of her government. More recently, Chancellor Angela Merkel has been argued to have a political style that is "*alternativlos*," using the absence of alternatives as a means of persisting with a policy and minimizing debate (Kurbjuweit, 2014). This political construction of an exhaustion of ideas obviously is very useful for those wanting to maintain the status quo, even if it may do long-term damage to policy discourse within the country.

If we return to the discussion of the role of path dependence in the persistence of policy ideas, Peters, Pierre and King (2005) have argued that path dependence may be explained in large part by the absence of alternatives. Change in the ideas influencing policy choices tends to come about through conflict over ideas, while older (and perhaps poor) ideas can persist without the presence of conflict. While policymakers and organizations may filter out ideas that challenge the conventional wisdom, those ideas have to exist to be filtered, and still may have some chance of surviving in the face of proponents of the status quo. Schrad's (2010) study of prohibition, for example, pointed out how institutions tended to narrow consideration of alternative policy options.

This strand of reasoning, focusing on the presence or absence of alternatives, has obvious affinities with the Advocacy Coalition Framework model (Sabatier and Weible, 2007). This model posits the existence of several alternative ideas for policy, represented by different coalitions attempting to shape or to maintain policy. Thus, there is competition over ideas central to policymaking. In the absence of alternative conceptions, the existing policy regime is likely to persist, albeit perhaps with the gradual changes now associated with historical institutionalism (Mahoney and Thelen, 2010). But without alternative ideas there will not be the "punctuated equilibrium" characteristic of the earlier conceptualizations of historical institutionalism (Steinmo et al., 1992).

Even though the conception of change within historical institutionalism has become more flexible than the original conception of punctuated equilibrium, there may still be some persistence of zombie ideas. For example, one of the conceptions of change now proposed is "layering," in which new ideas are added on top of old, with the older ideas and policies persisting. Another conception of change is "policy drift," meaning that a policy changes gradually. In both of these conceptions of policy change a zombie idea may be able to survive – and may even prosper, if the manner in which it drifts makes it more viable in a changed environment.

Similarly, the presence of alternatives can be related to the "frame reflection" as a mechanism for policy change and coordination (Schön and Rein, 1994). When policy ideas are entrenched in organizations, and those organizations have to find ways to work together, conflict is likely to ensue. But that conflict may also prevent moving forward with policy changes that can be beneficial to citizens. The process of reframing programs so that they can cooperate more effectively is clearly using ideas to shape policy, and it also potentially involves killing off some zombie ideas.

Thus, policy making is strongly affected by uncertainty and ambiguity. Hofstede et al. (2010) refer to March's term of uncertainty avoidance and develop the uncertainty avoidance index. They define it as the degree to which the members of a culture feel threatened by ambiguous or unknown situations. Among other things, this feeling is expressed in nervous stress and a need for predictability: a need for written and unwritten rules. When we look at the individuals and organizations who design public policies, we need to take into consideration the organizational background of the designers. According to Werner Jann (1983), for example, Germany is characterized as a formalized regulatory culture that is classified as fragmented, detailed, complicated, immobile, attached to the status quo and formalized. Accordingly, policy ideas may persist, because the success of any alternative policies is too uncertain. In other settings where policymaking is more open to innovation and even experimentation, older ideas, including zombie ideas, may be less dominant.

3.2.11 What is a Failure? What is the Evidence?

Failure, like many other aspects of politics and policy, is politically constructed (McConnell, 2015). Many public policies have produced results that can well be described as ambiguous. The outcomes may appear positive in general, yet the problem being addressed is not resolved totally, and there may also be negative unintended consequences (Baart, 1991) that reduce the overall positive impact of the policy. Thus, when a policy is implemented the outcomes may, in the eyes of its proponents, be definite successes, while in the eyes of its opponents the outcomes may be regarded as failures. With that ambiguity the policy ideas are able to survive, especially if (as mentioned previously) there is no clear alternative to the existing policy.

The ambiguity of policy results can be seen as a result of the political process involved in accepting policies. Even in authoritarian regimes, policies must be "oversold" as they are being legitimated by legislatures, or by an autocratic ruler, and that need for legitimation is even greater in democratic regimes. It is not sufficient to argue that we think this policy might work, or we hope it will, or even that we expect it to work. The policy must be put forward as *the* solution to the problem being addressed. This overselling sets a very high bar for success for a policy that is being implemented in a challenging and complex social setting.

If the standard for success of the policy becomes not amelioration of the problem but actual solution, success becomes less likely. Further, as has been demonstrated a number of times, solutions for policy problems tend to be short lived. As Aaron Wildavsky pointed out some time ago (2018), policies may be their own causes, and today's solution will be tomorrow's problem. For politicians, producing today's solution may be sufficient because with any luck they will be out of office and writing their memoirs when the negative consequences or declining effectiveness of their policy begin to manifest.

But regardless of the standard of success and failure being applied, the measurement of that success and failure will to some extent be socially constructed. Most policy programs have sufficiently ambiguous and multiple goals that it is difficult to argue for complete success or failure, and therefore those who wish the policy to persist may well be able to find some evidence to justify the perpetuation of the program. As noted, when discussing the conceptual and measurement issues raised by zombie ideas, policies may continue and policy ideas persist simply because their success or failure is in the eye of the beholder.

The importance of social and political construction for the maintenance of zombie ideas can be linked to several of the causes of persistence already mentioned. Perhaps most importantly, symbols can be used to help in the political construction of success and failure. In some instances, merely adopting a policy with a strong symbolic element may in itself be constructed as a success. If a frugal president or prime minister is able to overcome all the spendthrifts in the public sector and protect future generations from high levels of public debt, that may be considered a success – or at least constructed as a success.

3.2.12 Explaining Ghost Ideas

As mentioned, ghost ideas are ideas that appear promising but are never adopted by governments, and hence never have an opportunity to demonstrate whether they could be successful. Just as we want to know how bad ideas persist, we want to know why potentially good ideas are not given an opportunity to work. One simple answer to that question is that some good ideas may be blocked by inferior ideas that have become "ideas in good currency" (Schön, 2010) and are now the programmed response of government actors to a particular type of policy problem. These are the "locks" described by Blyth (2001) that prevent innovation.

Ghost ideas can also be explained by the absence of "windows of opportunity." In the multiple streams literature in public policy (Zahariadis, 2019) there is the argument that adopting policies becomes possible when problems, policy (and policy ideas) and politics converge to create a window of opportunity. This convergence can to some extent be facilitated by policy entrepreneurs (see Section 3.2.5), but this convergence is often more subject to random events than to interventions by political actors. Thus, ghost ideas may simply never experience the type of window they may need to be fully considered and adopted. And the apparent opening of a window may be insufficient to have ideas adopted. After each mass shooting in the United States opinion writers say that surely this is the time that national gun control laws will be adopted, but they never are – these windows are shut very quickly by the powerful political forces maintaining the status quo.

The *difficulties encountered by good ideas trying to become* policy may also be considered through the agenda-setting literature. Many ghost ideas address problems that are not on the systemic agenda of government, and hence are largely excluded until political change or a "focusing event" (Birkland and Wenement, 2016) brings the issue onto the systemic agenda. When the systemic agenda is altered, then these ideas may have a chance. Some ghost ideas are in policy domains that are already recognized by government as being on the systemic agenda, but those specific policy ideas have not yet been accepted as components of an active institutional agenda.

Table 2 Patterns of Explanation for Zombie Ideas

| | *Types of Explanation* | | |
	Elite	Organizational	Social
Specific Explanations			
Path Dependence		X	
Beliefs	X		
Symbolism			X
Politics and Power	X		
Policy Entrepreneurship	X		
Links to Individuals	X		
Blame Avoidance	X		
Filtering Information		X	
Biases	X		
Absence of Alternatives	X		

The above explanations for the persistence of zombie ideas can be linked to the three more general forms of explanation (Section 3.1). These linkages are shown in Table 2. This table demonstrates several important things about the explanations for zombie ideas. First, this table is intended to show major links between the main factors involved in explanation and the various individual explanations. If we were to attempt to identify every possible influence, then there might an "X" in every cell of the table. For example, none of the zombie ideas would be effective if there were not some minimal level of support in the society for the idea.

To expand our understanding of the linkages between the general types of explanation for zombie ideas and the more specific explanations, Table 3 contains an upper-case "X" for major influences and a lower case "x" for less significant influences. Again, we have been selective in how we assigned influence from the general explanatory factors, but this does give a somewhat more complete view of patterns of influence. In particular, it shows greater influence from organizational factors over the maintenance of zombie ideas than was shown in Table 2.

A second point arising from these tables is that the elite explanations appear to be the most important for understanding zombie ideas. This should perhaps be expected, given that policymaking is dominated by elite actors (political, administrative and expert). Even if the zombie ideas are widely held elsewhere, the elites are crucial for placing them on the operational agenda of the public sector. However, it may be difficult, at times, to distinguish the independent

Table 3 Patterns of Explanation for Zombie Ideas (Expanded Version)

	Types of Explanation		
	Elite	**Organizational**	**Social**
Specific Explanations			
Path Dependence	x	X	
Beliefs	X		
Symbolism		x	
Politics and Power	X		
Policy Entrepreneurship	X		
Links to Individuals	X		
Blame Avoidance	X		
Filtering Information		X	
Biases	X		
Absence of Alternatives	X		

effect of elites from the effects of the organizations within which those elites function, especially for the administrative elites, as demonstrated in part through Table 3. Individual elite members may be socialized through their involvement with organizations and learn the ideas that the organization considers "appropriate."

The nexus between elites and organizations may be becoming even more important for explanation of the persistence of zombie ideas as elites continue to become increasingly segmented and more linked to specific policy sectors. Governments have always been fragmented into specialized organizations (Bouckaert et al., 2010; Scott, 2019) but the specialization of elites has been argued to be increasing (Genieys, 2017). Therefore, the elites will be more tied to the specific organizations responsible for policies and will also be more prone to perpetuating zombie ideas that are favored by those organizations, and in the policy domain more generally.

4 The Uses of Zombie Ideas

The discussion to this point may have had something of a deus ex machina feeling about it. Zombie ideas exist and they persist because of relatively impersonal forces. But there is also agency in the use of zombie ideas, and political leaders may choose to employ them for a variety of purposes. And they may choose to advocate ideas even when they know they are imperfect. Like any set of policy ideas, zombie ideas can be used in multiple ways and for multiple reasons, and can also have different types of consequences for policy and for citizens as well as for policymakers.

As discussed throughout this Element, the obvious use of zombie ideas is to shape public policies. Many political leaders and members of advocacy groups who push for the utilization of these failed ideas as the foundation of policy-making truly believe in them and want to shape policies according to these ideas. Even if those leaders recognize that the policy idea has failed in the past, their commitment to it will lead them to continue it advocate it, assuming that it will work this time, given that it appears to be so "right" given their own views about public policy. Previous failures are assumed to have been the product of poor implementation, poor timing, implementation in the wrong context, or just poor luck.

In addition to being used genuinely to create a policy, a zombie idea can also be used to block other policy ideas that are inimical to the interests of the advocates of the zombie idea. If an older tried (if not true) idea is available to policymakers, it may be easier to adopt than a more innovative idea. This is especially true if the alternative idea does not fit as well with the dominant political culture, or the particular ideology of the government of the day. Thus, always having a set of ideas on the shelf that can be used to fill the space when an idea is required to support a policy can reduce innovation and block any significant change.

These older, familiar ideas may be especially useful for organizations within the public bureaucracy that want to defend their "turf" from other organizations, or from policy innovation that would upset their routines and their dominance of the policy domain (Bardach, 1996). For example, although many aspects of command and control regulation in environmental policy are less than efficient or effective, this form of intervention is familiar to policymakers and regulatory organizations know how to implement these policies. Therefore, they can be used as a means of forestalling the introduction of more innovative, and perhaps more effective, modes of control.

Third, zombie ideas, as may also be true for other policy ideas, can be used to build political coalitions. These coalitions may be created at the political level as well as at the organizational level. At the political level, political parties of the same general family may be able to coalesce around old, established policy ideas (even if not very effective) more readily than around more innovative ideas that any one of the parties may be advocating. Building the coalition then becomes accepting a policy idea as the lowest, and familiar, common denominator (Schapf, 1988). For organizations within the public bureaucracy, the zombie idea may be a means of building a coalition, or coordinating, with other organizations. We noted earlier that these ideas could be barriers to coordination if held strongly by one organization, but if more widely shared could also be coordinative.

Finally, zombie ideas can be a source of security in times of crisis. This is perhaps especially true in the early days of a crisis when there may not appear to be many alternatives available to government to confront the crisis. As the situation becomes more clearly defined and more appropriate policy alternatives become available it may, however, be difficult to replace the zombie idea that was perhaps intended to be merely a placeholder enabling government to make some sort of initial response. The literature on crisis management (Schneider, 2011) shows that the initial labeling of a crisis – referred to as "keynoting" – is important for determining how it will be dealt with subsequently.

5 How Do Ideas Become Zombies?

We have discussed a number of reasons for the persistence of zombie ideas, but we need also to think about how they became zombies in the first instance. No policy thinker or policy advocate wants to be pushing for a zombie idea, yet despite that many good ideas may become zombies over time. So how do ideas lose their capacity to produce positive outcomes and become part of the legion of continuing bad ideas?

The first (and simplest) answer is that some ideas were wrong from the minute they were first advocated, but for various reasons continue to be part of the repertoire of government policies. Policy ideas of this sort are often linked to political ideologies, or fundamental belief systems, and hence may not be grounded in any empirical evidence. One example mentioned earlier is "workfare," which may save money for government but has little or no evidence to support the idea that it gets recipients back to work. An even clearer example may be "abstinence only" sex education, which is grounded in religious beliefs and persists despite widespread evidence of negative outcomes (Beh and Diamond, 2006).

A second way in which policy ideas become zombie ideas is through changes in the social, economic or political environments that affect the policy domain. Policy ideas that work in one setting may become outmoded as the world changes around them, but individuals committed to the old ideas will persist in advocating them. One historical example might be the demise of the gold standard as governments had to face first World War I and then the Great Depression. Despite the long period since there was a gold standard for currency, some economists and politicians still want a return to it as a means of preventing deficit financing and of stabilizing exchange rates (Tamny, 2020). More recently, the COVID-19 pandemic has been argued to be changing a host of assumptions about public policy and public finance and has opened the policy agenda for a range of new options (Arango and Fuller, 2020).

A third reason that policy ideas may become zombie ideas is that policy drift (Mahoney and Thelen, 2010) occurs, and thus there are changing interpretations of what the ideas and the resultant policies mean, and how they should be implemented. One good example of attempts to create a zombie idea occurred in the attempts to make the American Social Security program obsolete by creating tax-subsidized private retirement plans (Hacker, 2004). Although full privatization was later proposed, the creation of benefits such as 401ks moved Social Security from a "retirement wage" for the society to something approaching a social transfer.[24] That being said, however, policy drift may also occur in a purposive and more systematic manner in order to prevent policy ideas from becoming zombie ideas (Carstensen and Matthijs, 2018).

Related to the idea of policy drift, policy ideas may become zombie ideas when policies designed as means become ends in themselves. This process of change can be seen most clearly with transparency. Transparency was devised as a means of increasing the accountability of the public sector and did some good in making the political process more visible. But, over time, it has become a political goal in its own right, and may, as already noted, have unintended negative consequences that were not considered when implementing more transparent political processes.

Finally, policy ideas may become zombies because public sector priorities, and definitions of policy success and failure, change. This route to becoming a zombie policy is most likely for policies that have clear and largely unitary goals. If the policy is intended to do one thing and fails to do it, then it is clearer that it has become a zombie than if the policy has multiple goals and one goal can be said to be being reached even if other goals are not. The workfare program is an example, having the goal of getting people into employment that appears never to have worked but may persist because it can achieve a secondary (and at times unstated) goal of saving government money, and the even less frequently stated goal of punishing the poor.

6 Hypotheses About the Likelihood of Zombie Ideas

As a means of summarizing the foregoing discussion, we are present a number of hypotheses about zombie ideas. These hypotheses are in principle testable, but the difficulties in measuring some of the variables involved, and the

---

[24] The actual method for producing the change was layering by adding other publicly supported retirement options in addition to Social Security, but the net effect of that layering was policy drift.

difficulties in differentiating results as the product of one independent variable or another, may make any systematic testing difficult. Still, these hypotheses do point to some of the key factors involved in the persistence of zombie ideas and may have some relevance for the survival of even more successful policy ideas.

H1 Policies for which there is no clear measure of failure will be more prone to zombie ideas.

If it is clear to observers, whether politicians, citizens or the media, that a policy is failing then it may be more difficult for that policy to survive, and for the ideas on which it was based to remain acceptable. For some policies the actual effects may be hidden or diffuse, and hence assessing the performance of the policy will be difficult.

H2 Policies with a long time lag between implementation and outcomes will be more prone to zombies.

One factor that may reduce the visibility of failure of a policy idea is a long lag between the policy being put into effect and the outcomes of the policy. If policymakers and citizens cannot readily observe the effects of their policies, they are likely to persist even if they fail. These sleeper effects can also mask the success of policies that initially may have appeared to be successful (Salamon, 1979).

H3 Policies that are more episodic – disaster, war – will be more prone to zombies than others.

Governments presumably are preparing for wars, disasters and other major episodic events constantly, but their ideas for coping with those crises are tested only infrequently. In the absence of any feedback from reality, decision-makers may rely on outmoded ideas – generals are said to always be preparing for the last war.

H4 Policy domains dominated by powerful, and monolithic, interest groups are more prone to zombie ideas than are others.

Public policies are influenced, or shaped, by interest groups. In a policy domain in which there is limited competition among interest groups, and the policy ideas which they advocate are rather similar, the survival of ideas to which those groups are committed is more probable, even if those ideas are zombies.

H5 The better institutionalized a policy, and the organizations delivering it, the more likely are zombie ideas to persist.

To the extent that an institution has become institutionalized, with its ideas and values widely accepted by its members (see March and Olsen, 1989), the policies of that institution, and the ideas undergirding them, are more likely to be zombies. In this case, there is likely to be little internal challenge to the ideas.

H6 In policy domains in which there are few alternative ideas about policy, or few alternative institutions for making policy, zombie ideas are more likely to persist.

Some policy domains have a livelier set of institutions pushing forward ideas for policy change than do others. While all contemporary policy domains have think tanks and academic departments working in their area, some are more densely populated with ideas than are others, and in the more densely populated areas zombie ideas will have a more difficult time surviving.

H7a Democratic political systems are less likely to have zombie ideas than autocratic political systems.

Democratic political systems tend to be more open to new ideas than do autocratic systems (Jacobs, 2011). In addition, elections may be contests over ideas for governing, with, at least in theory, poor ideas losing out to better ideas. We have already noted that there may be differences among types of democratic systems, but, in general, democratic systems will be better at winnowing out ideas.

H7b Nondemocratic systems are less likely to have zombie ideas than democratic political systems.

In contrast to hypothesis 7a, we could argue that democratic political systems politicians may be unwilling to advocate innovative ideas and to denigrate popular, if faulty, policy ideas because of public opinion and the need to avoid blame for policy failure. Autocratic leaders will have no such constraints and can make innovative policies almost at will. This does not mean that the new ideas will be successful, only that they will be new.

7 Conclusion

This Element is not about how or why policies fail, although it certainly has implications for understanding failures. Rather, it is about why policies and policy ideas that have demonstrably failed (leaving aside the caveats about such a bold statement) continue to reappear. Like the zombies of horror films, they cannot be killed off and continue to stalk the policy world. These ideas are perhaps more numerous than we might imagine and appear in a number of policy domains in a number of political systems. But why do policy-makers, and ordinary citizens, continue to assume the utility of old, tired ideas?

We hope we have made clear that there is no simple answer to that question. Rather, the promotion and perpetuation of zombie ideas is a game that any number of actors can play. The persistence of weak or unworkable ideas is not entirely a function of the machinations of political elites or policy advocates. These ideas require support from the public, especially in democratic regimes. If an idea does not resonate with the voters then it is unlikely to survive very long, or at a minimum the politicians advocating this idea may have a limited political life expectancy.

Further, the reasons for promoting these ideas are even more varied than the actors involved in promoting them. Sheer inertia often plays a role, especially when there is no ready alternative to continuing to make the same arguments again and again. But political power and the use of failed ideas to maintain that political power of a political party or a political leader can be central factors in the preservation of policy ideas. Zombie ideas also are maintained through ideologies and beliefs that may be difficult to dislodge, even when not success-ful in producing the desired, and assumed, results.

Yet, we need to acknowledge that policies and their success depend on their environments. Environments and contexts change. For this reason, it is crucial to keep in mind that a policy that has not worked out in the past is not by default going to fail again. The survival of zombie ideas has positive aspects. It's about the competition of ideas, which is crucial for functioning democra-cies. And given the swinging of the political pendulum, both of ideas and political parties, between Right and Left, it may be that ideas that we now treat with disdain may not only prevail but actually become effective in dealing with real policy issues.

Finally, although we have examined the most egregious cases of holding on to ideas because they are familiar and a part of the furnishings of the political world, there is an even larger question to be addressed about the persistence of policy ideas in general. Most policymaking appears rather conservative and tends to perpetuate existing patterns of doing the public's business even as the environment and the political landscape change. A good deal of the argument made herein would help us to understand why there is relatively little innovation in public policy. Government is often criticized for being slow to adapt and to innovate. Those critiques are at times just a stereotype, but they can also be true, and this Element helps us to understand the resistance to change.

The same arguments – blame avoidance, an absence of perceived alternatives to existing policies, political and ideological biases – that explain why zombie ideas persist may also explain why functional, even if perhaps suboptimal, policies also persist. Ideas that "work" may still not be the best possible options, and the various reasons outlined herein for the persistence of zombie ideas will also explain why there is not greater openness of policymakers to new and creative policy ideas. The logic of bounded rationality might argue that it is appropriate to continue with these suboptimal policies, given decision-making costs and the possibility of error, but this will also mean that policies that could be better are not adopted.

This Element illustrates various explanations for the survival of ideas. Against this background practitioners might find the study useful to explore reasons for policy failure. Furthermore, policymakers could use the study in order to understand why certain ideas remain ghost ideas and do not pass a certain stage in the policy process. But perhaps most importantly, this Element should illustrate the significance of ideas in policymaking, and the positive and negative effects that ideas can have on achieving the goals of policymakers.

And even more generally, the study of zombie ideas can serve as a means of understanding policy change, or the absence there of. The challenge for public policymakers, then, is to find ways – careful, well-informed ways – to move away from the status quo to find better ways of serving the public. The common stereotype of the public sector as resistant to change may be true in some instances, or even in many instances, and understanding how poor ideas persist can help us to understand this resistance to change and perhaps overcome it.

References

Allison, G. T. and P. Zelikow (1999) *Essence of Decision: Explaining the Cuban Missile Crisis* (New York: Longman).

Altenburg, T. and W. Lütkenhorst (2015) *Industrial Policy in Developing Countries: Failing Markets, Weak States* (Cheltenham: Edward Elgar).

Anderson, D. M. and D. I. Rees (2011) Medical Marijuana Laws, Alcohol Consumption and Traffic Fatalities (Bonn: IZA). IZA Discussion Paper 6112.

Arango, T. and T. Fuller (2020) Why Liberal Californians Don't Want to Go Back to Normal, *New York Times*, May 4.

Bach, T. and K. Wegrich (2019). Blind Spots, Biased Attention, and the Politics of Non Coordination, in T. Bach and K. Wegrich, eds., *The Blind Spots of Public Bureaucracy and the Politics of Non-Coordination*. (London: Palgrave Macmillan).

Baert, P. (1991) Unintended Consequences: Typology and Examples, *International Sociology* 6, 201–10.

Bardach, E. (1996) Turf Barriers in Inter-Agency Collaboration, in D. F. Kettl and H. B. Milward, eds., *The State of Public Management* (Baltimore, MD: Johns Hopkins University Press).

Bardach, E. (1997) *Getting Agencies to Work Together* (Washington, DC: The Brookings Institution).

Bason, C. (2016) *Design for Policy* (London: Routledge)

Beh, H. G. and M. Diamond (2006) The Failure of Abstinence-Only Education: Minors Have a Right to Honest Talk About Sex, *Columbia Journal of Gender and Law* 15, 12–49.

Behague, D., C. Tawiah, M. Rosato, T. Some and J. Morrison (2009) Evidence-based Policymaking: The Implications of Globally Applicable Research for Context-Specific Problem-Solving in Developing Countries, *Social Science and Medicine* 69, 1529–46.

Béland, D. (2019) *How Ideas and Institutions Shape the Politics of Public Policy* (Cambridge: Cambridge University Press).

Béland, D. and R. H. Cox (2011) *Ideas and Politics in Social Science Research* (New York: Oxford University Press).

Béland, D. and R. H. Cox (2013) Valence, Policy Ideas, and the Rise of Sustainability, *Governance* 26, 307–28.

Béland, D. and R. H. Cox (2016) Ideas as Coalition Magnets: Coalition Building, Policy Entrepreneurship and Power Relations, *European Journal of Public Policy* 23, 428–45.

Béland, D. and M. Howlett (2016) How Solutions Chase Problems: Instrument Constituencies in the Policy Process, *Governance* 25, 393–409.

Bellé, N., P. Cantarelli and P. Belardinelli (2018) Prospect Theory Goes Public: Experimental Evidence on Cognitive Biases in Public Policy and Management Decisions, *Public Administration Review* 78, 828–40.

Berger, P. and T. Luckmann (1966) *The Social Construction of Reality* (New York: Anchor Books).

Birkinshaw, P. (2006) Transparency as a Human Right, in C. Hood and D. Heald, eds. *Transparency: The Key to Better Government?* (Oxford: Oxford University Press).

Birkland, T. A. and M. K. Warnement (2016) Refining the Idea of Focusing Events in the Multiple-Steams Framework, in R. Zohlnhöfer and F. W. Rüb, eds. *Decision-Making Under Ambiguity and Time Constraints* (Colchester: ECPR Press).

Blyth, M. (2001) The Transformation of the Swedish Model: Economic Ideas. Distributional Conflict and Institutional Change, *World Politics* 54, 1–26.

Blyth, M. (2013) *Austerity: The History of a Dangerous Idea* (Oxford: Oxford University Press).

Bouckaert, G., B. G. Peters and K. Verhoest (2010) *The Coordination of Public Sector Organizations: Shifting Patterns of Public Management* (London: Macmillan).

Bovens, M. A. P and P. 't Hart (1998) *Understanding Policy Fiascoes* (New Brunswick, NJ: Transaction).

Bovens, M. A. P. And P. 't Hart (2016) Revisiting the Study of Policy Failure, *Journal of European Public Policy* 23, 653–66.

Cairney, P. (2016) *The Politics of Evidence-based Policymaking* (London: Macmillan).

Campbell, D. T and J. C. Stanley (1963) *Experimental and Quasi-Experimental Design for Research* (Chicago: Rand-McNally).

Campbell, J. R. (2002) Ideas, Polities and Public Policy, *Annual Review of Sociology* 28, 21–38.

Campbell, J. R. and M. P. Anderson (2001) Identifying Shifts in Policy Regimes: Cluster and Interrupted Time-series Analyses of US Income Taxes, *Social Science History* 25, 37–65.

Carstensen, M. B. and M. Matthijs (2018) Of Paradigms and Power: British Economic Policy Making Since Thatcher, *Governance* 31, 431–47.

Carter, P. (2012) Policy as Palimpsest, *Policy & Politics* 40, 423–43.

Cashore, B. and I. Nathan (2019) Good Governance Gone Bad: Assessing the Impact of Transnational Market-Driven Interventions Designed to Make

"Weak States" Stronger (Unpublished Paper, Department of Political Science, Yale University).

Cobb, R. W. and C. D. Elder (1971) The Politics of Agenda-Building: An Alternative Perspective for Modern Democratic Theory, *Journal of Politics* 33, 892–915.

Coy, P. (2018) Trump's Tax Cuts Made a Difference in 2018, Just not the One Backers Were Hoping For, *Bloomberg Businessweek*, December 13 www .bloomberg.com/news/articles/2018-12-13/trump-s-tax-cuts-had-an-impact-but-not-the-one-backers-hoped-for

Cyert, R. and J. G. March (1963) *A Behavioral Theory of the Firm* (Englewood Cliffs, NJ: Prentice-Hall).

Daigneault, P.-M. (2014) Reassessing the Concept of Policy Paradigm: Aligning Ontology and Methodology in Policy Studies, *Journal of European Public Policy* 21, 453–69.

Davenport, C, and H. Tabuchi (2019) Automakers, Rejecting Trump Pollution Rule, Strike a Deal with California, *New York Times*, July 25.

Davis, K. and C. Schoen (1978) *Health and the War on Poverty: A Ten-Year Appraisal* (Washington, DC: The Brookings Institution).

Dimaggio, P. and W. Powell (1991) The Iron Cage Revisited: Institutional Isomorphism and Collective Rationality in Organizational Fields, *American Sociological Review* 48, 147–60.

Dodson, D. (2019) Political Parties are Monopolies, *The New York Times*, May 21.

Ellis, J. (1975) *The Social History of the Machine Gun* (New York: Pantheon).

Erkkilä, T. (2012) *Government Transparency: Impacts and Unintended Consequences* (London: Macmillan).

Fung, A, M. Graham and D. Weil (2007) *Full Disclosure: The Perils and Promise of Transparency* (Cambridge: Cambridge University Press).

Gentile, G. P. (2001) *How Effective is Strategic Bombing?: Lessons Learned from World War II to Kosovo* (New York: New York University Press).

Genieys, W. (2017) *The New Custodians of the State: Programmatic Elites in French Society* (London: Routledge).

Gill, A. (2014). Mexico, in J. Kopstein, M. Lichtbach, and S. Hanson, eds., *Comparative Politics* (Cambridge: Cambridge University Press).

Goodsell, C. T. (2011), *Mission Mystique: Belief Systems in Public Agencies* (Washington, DC: CQ Press).

Green, E. L and D. Goldstein (2019) Reading Scores on National Exams Decline in Half the States, *New York Times*, October 30 (updated December 5).

Greenberg, D. and A. Cebulla (2008) The Cost-Effectiveness of Welfare-to-Work Programs: A Meta-Analysis, *Public Budgeting and Finance* 28, 112–45.

Hacker, J. S. (2004) Privatizing Risk Without Privatizing the Welfare State: The Hidden Politics of Social Policy Retrenchment in the United States. *American Political Science Review* 98, 243–60.

Hale, W. G., H. Gelfond, A. Krupkin, M. J. Mazur and E. Toder (2018) *Effects of the Tax Cuts and Jobs Act: A Preliminary Analysis* (Washington, DC: Tax Policy Center).

Hall, P. A. (1993) Policy Paradigms, Social Learning, and the State: The Case of Economic Policymaking in Britain, *Comparative Politics* 25, 275–96.

Hall, P. A., and D. W. Soskice (2001) *Varieties of Capitalism: The Institutional Foundations of Comparative Advantage* (Oxford: Oxford University Press).

Hastings, M. (2018) *Vietnam: An Epic Tragedy 1945–1975* (New York: Harper).

Hay, C. (2011) Ideas and the Construction of Interests, in D. Béland and R. H. Cox, eds., *Ideas and Politics in Social Science Research* (New York: Oxford University Press).

Hodgson, G. M. (2004) Reclaiming Habit for Institutional Economics, *Journal of Economic Psychology* 25, 651–60.

Hofstede, G., G. J. Hofstede and M. Minkov (2010) *Cultures and Organizations: Software of the Mind: Intercultural Cooperation and its Importance for Survival*. 3rd ed. (New York: McGraw-Hill).

Hogwood, B. W. and B. G. Peters (1985) *The Pathology of Public Policy* (Oxford: Oxford University Press).

Homedes, N. and A. Ugalde (2005) Why Neoliberal Health Reforms Have Failed in Latin America, *Health Policy* 71, 83–96.

Hood, C. (1984) *The Tools of Government* (Chatham, NJ: Chatham House).

Hood, C. (2011) *The Blame Game: Spin, Bureaucracy and Self-Preservation in Government* (Princeton, NJ: Princeton University Press).

Houghton, D. P. (1996) The Role of Analogical Reasoning in Novel Foreign Policy Situations, *British Journal of Political Science* 26, 523–52.

Hurley, A. F. (1975) *Billy Mitchell: Crusader for Air Power* (Bloomington: Indiana University Press).

Innes, J. E. and D. E. Booher (2018) *Planning with Complexity: An Introduction to Collaborative Rationality for Public Policy*. 2nd ed. (London: Routledge).

Irwin, N. (2020) America is addicted to Using the Tax Code to Fix its Problems, *New York Times* March 6.

Jacobs, A. N. (2011) *Governing for the Long Term: Democracy and the Politics of Investment* (Cambridge: Cambridge University Press).

Jacobs, J. B. (2002) *Can Gun Control Work?* (Oxford: Oxford University Press).

James, W. (1890) *Principles of Psychology* (New York: Henry Holt).

Janis, I. (1991) Groupthink, in E. Griffin, ed. *A First Look at Communication Theory* (New York: McGraw Hill).

Jann, W. (1983), *Staatliche Programme und Verwaltungskultur. Bekämpfung des Drogenmissbrauchs und der Jugendarbeitslosigkeit in Schweden, Großbritannien und der Bundesrepublik Deutschland im Vergleich.* (Opladen: Westdeutscher Verlag).

Jann, W., and G. Wewer, (1998): Helmut Kohl und der schlanke Staat. Eine verwaltungspolitische Bilanz, in G. Wewer, eds. *Bilanz der Ära Kohl* (Opladen: Westdeutscher Verlag).

Jones, B. D. (1999) Bounded Rationality, *Annual Review of Political Science* 2, 297–321.

Jones, B. D. and W. Williams (2008) *The Politics of Bad Ideas: The Great Tax Cut Delusion and the Decline of Good Government in America* (New York: Longman).

Jordan, A. J. and J. R. Turnpenny (2015) *The Tools of Policy Formulation* (Cheltenham: Edward Elgar).

Judt, T. (2010) *Ill Fares the Land* (New York: Penguin).

Kaiser Health Network (2019) *KHN Morning Briefing: Medicaid Work Requirements*, May 16.

King, A. and I. Crewe (2013) *The Blunders of Our Governments* (London: Oneworld).

Kingdon, J. W. (2003) *Agendas, Alternatives and Public Policy*, 2nd ed. (New York: Longman).

Kleck, G. (2012) Gun Control After Heller and McDonald: What Cannot Be Done and What Can be Done, *Fordham Urban Law Journal* 39, 1383–420.

Koppl, R. (2018) *Expert Failure* (Cambridge: Cambridge University Press).

Krugman, P. (2019) The Zombie Style in American Politics: Why Bad Ideas Just Won't Stay Dead, *The New York Times*, April 29.

Krugman, P. (2020) *Arguing with Zombies: Economics, Politics and the Fight for a Better Future* (New York: W. W. Norton).

Kuhn, T. S. (1962) *The Structure of Scientific Revolutions* (Chicago: University of Chicago Press).

Kurbjuweit, D. (2014) *Alternativlos: Merkl, die Deutschen und das Ende der Politik* (Munich: Carl Hanser Verlag).

Lacorne, D. (2016) *Les frontières de la tolérance* (Paris: Gallimard).

Leeuw, F. L. (1991) Policy Theories, Knowledge Utilization, and Evaluation, *Knowledge and Policy* 4, 73–91.

Legro, J. W. (2000) The Transformation of Policy Ideas, *American Journal of Political Science* 44, 419–32.

Levin, K., B. Cashore, S. Bernstein and G. Auld (2012) Overcoming the Tragedy of Super Wicked Problems: Constraining our Future Selves to Ameliorate Global Climate Change. *Policy Sciences* 45, 2, 123–52.

Li, W. And Tao Yang, D. (2005) The Great Leap Forward: Anatomy of a Central Planning Disaster, *Journal of Political Economy* 113, 840–77.

Lijphart, A. (2012) *Patterns of Democracy: Government Forms and Performance in Thirty-Six Countries, 2nd. Ed*. (New Haven, CT: Yale University Press).

Linder, S. H. And B. G. Peters (1989) Instruments of Government: Perceptions and Contexts, *Journal of Public Policy* 9, 35–58.

Linder, S. H. and B. G. Peters (1992) The Study of Policy Instruments, *Policy Currents* 2, 1–7.

Linderman, J. (2019) 688,000 will Lose Food Stamp Benefits Under Trump's New Work Rule, *Los Angeles Times*, December 4.

Mahoney, J, and K. Thelen (2010) *Explaining Institutional Change: Ambiguity, Agency and Power* (Cambridge: Cambridge University Press).

Malesky, E., P. Schuler and A, Tran (2012) The Adverse Effects of Sunshine: A Field Experiment on Transparency in an Authoritarian Legislature, *American Political Science Review* 106, 762–76.

Maor, M. (2012) Policy Over-reaction, *Journal of Public Policy* 32, 231–59.

March, J. G. (1996) Continuity and Change in Theories of Organizational Action, *Administrative Science Quarterly* 41, 278–87.

March, J. G. and J. P. Olsen (1989) *Rediscovering Institutions* (New York: Free Press).

March, J. G. And J. P. Olsen (2011) The Logic of Appropriateness, in R. E. Goodin, ed., *Oxford Handbook of Political Science* (Oxford: Oxford University Press).

McConnell, A. (2010) *Understanding Policy Success: Rethinking Public Policy* (Basingstoke: Macmillan).

McConnell, A. (2015) What is Policy Failure? A Primer to Help Navigate the Maze, *Public Policy and Administration* 30, 221–42.

McConnell, A, (2019) The Use of Placebo Ideas to Escape Policy Traps, *European Journal of Public Policy* 27, 7, 957–76.

McIntyre A. (1992) Utilitarianism and Cost-Benefit Analysis: An Essay on the Relevance of Moral Philosophy to Bureaucratic Theory, in J. M. Gilroy and M. Wade, eds., *The Moral Dimension of Public Policy Choice* (Pittsburgh: University of Pittsburgh Press).

Mehta, J. (2011) The Varied Role of Ideas in Politics: From "Whether" to "How," in D. Béland and R. H. Cox, eds., *Ideas and Politics in Social Science Research* (New York: Oxford University Press).

Moynihan, D. P., and S. Lavertu (2012). Does Involvement in Performance Management Routines Encourage Performance Information Use? Evaluating GPRA and PART. *Public Administration Review* 72, 592–602.

Mintrom, M. And J. Luetjens (2017) Policy Entrepreneurs and Problem Framing: The Case of Climate Change, *Environment and Planning C: Politics and Space* 35, 1362–77.

Mintrom, M. and P. Norman (2009) Policy Entrepreneurship and Policy Change, *Policy Studies Journal* 37, 649–67.

Nguyen, T. (2020) Coronavirus Gets a Promising Drug but MAGAworld Isn't Buying It, *Politico*, May 2 www.politico.com/search?q=coronavirus+gets+a+promising+drug

Peacock, A. (1989) The Rise and Fall of the Laffer Curve, in D. Bös and B. Felderer, eds., *The Political Economy of Progressive Taxation* (Heidelberg: Springer).

Peneder, M. (2017) Competitiveness and Industrial Policy: From the Rationalities of Failure towards the Ability to Evolve, *Cambridge Journal of Economics* 41, 829–58.

Peters, B. G. (2014) Information and Governing: Cybernetic Models of Governance, in D. Levi-Faur, ed., *The Oxford Handbook of Governance* (Oxford: Oxford University Press).

Peters, B. G. (2016) *Advanced Introduction to Public Policy* (Cheltenham: Edward Elgar).

Peters, B. G. (2018) *Policy Problems and Policy Design* (Cheltenham: Edward Elgar).

Peters, B. G. (2021) Can We Be So Casual about Being Causal? *Journal of Comparative Policy Analysis* [forthcoming].

Peters, B. G., J. Pierre and D. S. King (2005) The Politics of Path Dependency: Political Conflict in Historical Institutionalism, *Journal of Politics* 67, 1275–300.

Pfeffer, J. (2005) Why Do Bad Management Theories Persist?: A Comment on Ghoshal, *Academy of Management Learning & Education* 4, 96–100.

Pierce, J. J., S. Siddiki, M. D. Jones, K. Schumacher, A. Pattison and H. Peterson (2004) Social Construction and Policy Design: A Review of Past Applications, *Policy Studies Journal* 42, 1–29.

Pierson, P. (2000) Increasing Returns, Path Dependence and the Study of Politics, *American Political Science Review* 94, 251–67.

Quaid, M. (2002) *Workfare: Why Good Social Policy Ideas Go Bad* (Toronto: University of Toronto Press).

Quiggin, J. (2013) *Zombie Economics: How Dead Ideas Still Walk Among Us* (Princeton, NJ: Princeton University Press).

Riddell, P. (2019) *15 Minutes of Power: The Uncertain Life of British Ministers* (London: Profile Books).

Riley, C. L. (2019) For Labour the 2019 Election Echoes "the Longest Suicide Note in History," *Post Everything (The Washington Post)*, www.washington post.com/outlook/2019/12/14/labour-election-echoes-longest-suicide-note-history/

Röber, M. (2018) Outsourcing und Privatisierung. In R. Voigt, ed., *Handbuch Staat* (Wiesbaden: Springer VS). https://doi.org/10.1007/978-3-658-20744-1_94

Roberts, A. (2006) Dashed Expectations: Government Adaptation to Transparency Rules, in C. Hood and D. Heald, eds. *Transparency: The Key to Better Government?* (Oxford: Oxford University Press).

Rocco, P. and C. Thurston (2014) From Metaphor to Measures: Observable Indicators of Gradual Institutional Change, *Journal of Public Policy* 34, 35–62.

Rochefort, D. A. and R. W. Cobb (1994) *The Politics of Problem Definition: Shaping the Policy Agenda* (Lawrence: University Press of Kansas).

Rodrik, D. (2014) When Ideas Trump Interests: Preferences, Worldviews and Policy Innovations, *Journal of Economic Perspectives* 28, 189–208.

Rose, R. (1976) *The Problem of Party Government* (London: Macmillan).

Rosenbluth, F. And I Shapiro (2018) *Responsible Parties: Saving Democracy From Itself* (New Haven, CT: Yale University Press).

Rosenthal, M. R. (2009) What Works in Market-oriented Health Policy, *New England Journal of Medicine* 360, 2157–60.

Sabatier, P. A. and C. M. Weible (2007) The Advocacy Coalition Framework, in C. M. Weible, ed., *Theories of the Policy Process* (Boulder, CO: Westview Pres).

Salamon, L. M. (1979) The Time Dimension in Policy Evaluation: The Case of New Deal Land Reform, *Public Policy*, 27, 2, 129–83.

Sarigil, Z. (2015) Showing the Path to Path Dependence: The Habitual Path, *European Political Science Review* 7, 221–42.

Scharpf, F. W. (1988) The Joint Decision Trap: Lessons from German Federalism and European Integration, *Public Administration* 66, 239–78.

Schmidt, V A. (2016) The Resilience of "Bad Ideas" in Eurozone Crisis Discourse, Even as Rival Ideas Inform Changing Practice. Paper presented at 23rd Conference of Europeanists.

Schmitter, P. C. (1974) Still the Century of Corporatism? *Review of Politics* 36, 85–131.

Schneider, S. K. (2011) *Dealing with Disaster: Public Management in Crisis Situations*, 2nd ed. (Armonk, NY: M. S. Sharpe).

Schön, D. A. (2010) Government as a Learning System, in C. Blackmore, ed., *Social Learning Systems and Communities of Practice* (London: Springer).

Schön, D. A. and M. Rein (1994) *Frame Reflection: Solving Intractable Policy Disputes* (Cambridge: MIT Press).

Schrad, M. L. (2010) *The Political Power of Bad Ideas: Networks, Institutions and the Global Prohibition Wave* (Oxford: Oxford University Press).

Schröder, M. (2014) *Varianten des Kapitalismus – Die Unterschiede liberaler und koordinierter Marktwirtschaften* (Wiesbaden: Springer VS).

Schulman, P. R. (1980) *Large-Scale Policymaking* (Greenwood, CT: Praeger).

Schumacher, G. and K. Van Kersbergen (2016) Do Mainstream Parties Adapt to the Welfare Chauvinism of Populist Parties? *Party Politics* 22, 300–12.

Schut, F. T. And W. P. M. M. Van de Ven (2011) Effects of Purchaser Competition in the Dutch Health System: Is the Glass Half Full or Half Empty? *Health Economics, Policy and Law* 6, 109–23.

Scott, I. (2019) Governing by Silos, in B. G. Peters and I. Thynne, eds., *Oxford Research Encyclopedia in Public Administration* (Oxford: Oxford University Press).

Seibel, W. (1992) *Funktionaler Dilettantismus: Erfolgreich scheiternde Organisationen im "Dritten Sektor" zwischen Markt und Staat*, 2nd ed. (Baden-Baden: Nomos).

Séville, A. (2017) From "One Right Way" to "One Ruinous Way": Discursive Shifts in "There is no Alternative," *European Political Science Review* 9, 449–70.

Shapiro, I. (2017) Collusion in Restraint of Democracy: Against Political Deliberation, *Daedalus* 146, 3, 77–84.

Sherman, L. W. (2003) Misleading Evidence and Evidence-Led Policy: Making the Social Sciences More Experimental, *Annals of the American Academy of Political and Social Science* 589, 6–19.

Soskice, D. W. (1999). Divergent Production Regimes: Coordinated and Uncoordinated Market Economies in the 1980s and 1990s. In H. Kitschelt, P. Lange, G. Marks, and J. Stephens, eds., *Continuity and Change in Contemporary Capitalism* (Cambridge: Cambridge University Press). DOI:10.1017/CBO9781139175050.006

Steinmo, S., K. Thelen and F. Longstreth (1992) *Structuring Politics: Historical Institutionalism in Comparative Analysis* (Cambridge: Cambridge University Press).

Stubbs, R. (2009) Whatever Happened to the East Asian Developmental State?: The Unfolding Debate, *The Pacific Review* 22, 1–22.

Sydow, J., G. Schreyögg and J. Koch (2009) Organizational Path Dependence: Opening the Black Box, *Academy of Management Review* 34, 689–709.

't Hart, P. (1990) *Groupthink in Government: A Study of Small Groups and Policy Failure* (Amsterdam: Swets & Zeitlinger).

Tamny, J. (2020) A Few Questions for the Many Critics of the Gold Standard, *Real Clear Markets*, February 25. www.realclearmarkets.com/articles/2020/02/24/a_few_questions_for_the_many_critics_of_the_gold_standard_485148.html

Tang, W. (2016) *Populist Authoritarianism: Chinese Political Culture and Regime Sustainability* (Oxford: Oxford University Press).

Thompson, V. A. (1977) *Modern Organizations*, 2nd ed. (Tuscaloosa: University of Alabama Press).

Vedung, E. (2013) Six Models of Evaluation, in E. Araral, S. Fritzen, M. Howlett, M. Ramesh and X. Wu, eds., *Routledge Handbook of Public Policy* (London: Routledge).

Walt, S. M. (2005) The Relationship Between Theory and Policy in International Relations, *Annual Review of Political Science* 8, 23–48.

Weaver, R. K. (1986) The Politics of Blame Avoidance, *Journal of Public Policy* 6, 371–98.

Weyland, K. (2008) Toward a new Theory of Institutional Change, *World Politics* 60, 281–304.

Wildavsky, A. (2018[1980]) Policy as its Own Cause, in A. Wildavsky, *The Art and Craft of Policy Analysis* (London: Macmillan).

Winters, J. A. and B. I. Page (2009) Oligarchy in the United States? *Perspectives on Politics* 7, 731–51.

Wollmann, H. (2002) Verwaltungspolitische Reformdiskurse und verläufe im internationalen Vergleich, in K. König, ed., *Deutsche Verwaltung in der Wende zum 21. Jahrhundert* (Baden-Baden: Nomos).

Zahariadis, N. (2019) The Multiple Streams Framework: Structure, Limitations, Prospects, in C. M. Weible and P. A. Sabatier, eds., *Theories of the Policy Process*, 4th ed. (Boulder, CO: Westview Press).

Zimmermann, N. (2017) German issues in a nutshell: Hartz IV, *Deutsche Welle*.

Cambridge Elements ☰

Public Policy

M. Ramesh
National University of Singapore (NUS)
M. Ramesh is UNESCO Chair on Social Policy Design at the Lee Kuan Yew School of Public Policy, NUS. His research focuses on governance and social policy in East and Southeast Asia, in addition to public policy institutions and processes. He has published extensively in reputed international journals. He is Co-editor of *Policy and Society and Policy Design and Practice*.

Michael Howlett
Simon Fraser University, British Colombia
Michael Howlett is Burnaby Mountain Professor and Canada Research Chair (Tier 1) in the Department of Political Science, Simon Fraser University. He specialises in public policy analysis, and resource and environmental policy. He is currently editor-in-chief of *Policy Sciences* and co-editor of the *Journal of Comparative Policy Analysis, Policy and Society* and *Policy Design and Practice*.

Xun WU
Hong Kong University of Science and Technology
Xun WU is Professor and Head of the Division of Public Policy at the Hong Kong University of Science and Technology. He is a policy scientist whose research interests include policy innovations, water resource management and health policy reform. He has been involved extensively in consultancy and executive education, his work involving consultations for the World Bank and UNEP.

Judith Clifton
University of Cantabria
Judith Clifton is Professor of Economics at the University of Cantabria, Spain. She has published in leading policy journals and is editor-in-chief of the *Journal of Economic Policy Reform*. Most recently, her research enquires how emerging technologies can transform public administration, a forward-looking cutting-edge project which received €3.5 million funding from the Horizon2020 programme.

Eduardo Araral
National University of Singapore (NUS)
Eduardo Araral is widely published in various journals and books and has presented in forty conferences. He is currently Co-Director of the Institute of Water Policy at the Lee Kuan Yew School of Public Policy, NUS and is a member of the editorial board of *Journal of Public Administration Research and Theory* and the board of the Public Management Research Association.

About the series

Elements in Public Policy is a concise and authoritative collection of assessments of the state of the art and future research directions in public policy research, as well as substantive new research on key topics. Edited by leading scholars in the field, the series is an ideal medium for reflecting on and advancing the understanding of critical issues in the public sphere. Collectively, it provides a forum for broad and diverse coverage of all major topics in the field while integrating different disciplinary and methodological approaches.

Cambridge Elements ≡

Public Policy

9 781108 926034